BRAIN
BUILDING
GAMES
WITH WORDS & NUMBERS (mostly)

BRAIN
BUILDING
GAMES

WITH WORDS *&* NUMBERS (mostly)

by
Allen D. Bragdon
and
David Gamon, Ph.D.

A DIVISION OF
ALLEN D. BRAGDON PUBLISHERS, INC.
CAPE COD & SAN FRANCISCO

Brainwaves Books, a Division of
Allen D. Bragdon Publishers, Inc.
252 Great Western Road
South Yarmouth, MA 02664

Design and editorial production: Carolyn Zellers
Exercise editing: Wallace Exman
Puzzle graphics formatting: David Zellers
Performance Tips text rewrite: Melissa Pendleton
Proofreader: Vida Morris

Drawings by Malcolm Wells
Cover design by Carolyn Zellers.

Some puzzle concepts were first published in a column called " Playspace" that was
created by Allen Bragdon in the 1980's for global syndication by The New York Times.
Some images copyright © 2001 www.arttoday.com. Some images reproduced with
permission of LifeArt Collection Images, copyright © 1989-99 TechPOOL Studios,
Cleveland, OH. Drawing on page 119 copyright 1998 by Nedjelja/Sarajevo.

Library of Congress Catalog Number: 2001117268
ISBN 0-916410-78-1

Printed in the United States of America

01 02 03   10 9 8 7 6 5 4 3 2 1

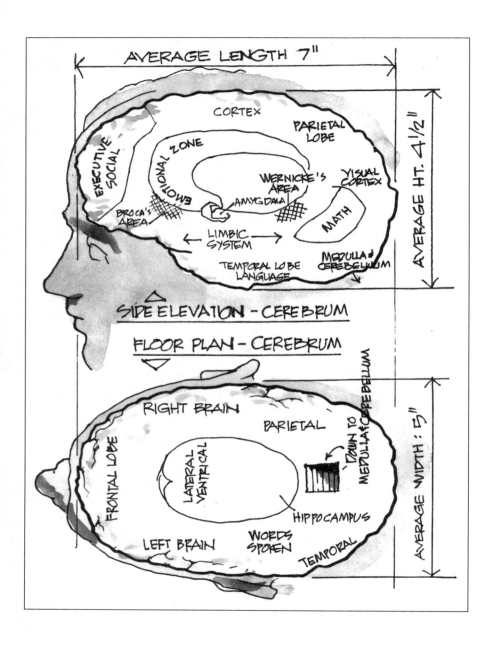

Contents

INTRODUCTION   8

SECTION ONE: 11 - 42
Executive Function
It solves problems by arranging data in cause-effect order to test for its usefulness in achieving a selected goal — discarding the useless as it goes.
14 Mental Exercises

SECTION TWO: 43 - 66
Memory Functions
Memory is the mother of thinking. Focus is its father. Exercises like these build powers of concentration. Jobs that draw on memory, constantly, enlarge the hippocampus.
10 Mental Exercises

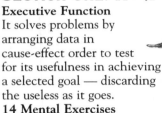

SECTION THREE: 67 - 110
Computational Function
It fits relative values into rule-driven structures. In that sense, math is a language of precisely measurable relationships that guide the mind to conclusions, some of which are surprises, just as its sister art, music, does.
20 Mental Exercises

SECTION FOUR: 111 - 134
Spatial Function

Rotating shapes in the mind's eye is a born skill. Architects and left-handers are usually better equipped for it. Men use it to read maps upside down, pack car trunks and build empires.
10 Mental Exercises

SECTION FIVE: 135 - 186
Language Function
Working left-hemisphere word tasks releases pleasure-feeling neurotransmitters. And it builds vocabulary too. Good deal?
24 Mental Exercises

SECTION SIX: 187 - 210
Social/Emotional Functions
The most human part of the brain spends most of its time telling instinct systems to cool it. Gender stuff here.
6 Mental Exercises and Tests

SOLUTIONS   211 - 221

PERFORMANCE TIPS   222

Congratulations! You have decided to take charge of your brain's future. That is the hard part. Our contribution to that effort is to create exercises in interesting puzzle formats. We are also going to tell you how the six cognitive systems that work hardest for you in real-world situations can be made to do their best work. We call these functions the *Executive, Memory, Computation, Spatial, Language* and *Social/Emotional*. Those are the ones that make you excel at work, build a useful store of memories, plan for and live an interesting old age.

Permit us some straight talk about your second most valuable possession. Your brain began to slow down as soon as its original blueprint finished unfolding in your mid 20s. It has lost capacity at the same rate every year since, and it will continue to do so. Symptoms of slowing down — from "senior moments" to Alzheimer's — are simply signs of the cumulative effects of continuing loss that have begun to show up in your outward behavior.

The good news is that you can *do* something about that. You took the first step when you picked up this book. It is designed to help you slow down the slowing down. There are no pills or vaccines yet to boost your smarts with no effort. In ten years some memory-enhancing pills will be tested, approved and sold. Now, targeted exercise is as good for your brain as for your muscles and cardio-pulmonary systems.

Try one exercise each day. Start with the easy ones. If you get stuck, don't quit on that exercise. Use the "Hint" printed in small type, upside down at the bottom of the page. Rotate from chapter to chapter during each week. Think of that daily routine as being like sets of physical exercises for different muscle-groups. There are enough exercises here for a three-month training course. When you have finished the book try one of the first ones you did again. Even if you have forgotten the answer you will be surprised at how easy it seems.

Each day you will be able to learn something about how the human brain works when it solves problems. We call these performance tips "didjaknows" because many of them will come as a surprise. Yet we have selected them from cutting-edge neuroscientific research results, many of them from research published since the millennium. Often you can apply them directly to real life situations to improve performance. Some will confirm a sense you have had all along, on your own, about how the brain gets things done. In the back of this book we compiled these tips into a "Performance Tips" title-list so you can quickly look one up again if you want to tell someone else about it. (They make wonderful conversation-starters at parties.)

Together, the exercises and the performance tips will help you in three, quite different, ways. First, they will make you more effectively aware that you can actually control much of what goes on in your brain. You can improve the hand you were dealt. Second, they will teach you strategies for seeing problems in ways that suggest solutions. The different puzzle formats can be applied to real-world problems. Third, you will be growing stronger brain cells. Yes, when you make cells work they will physically grow new connectors, called *dendrites* and *axons*, that allow them to pass along signals from cell to cell. Like anything else, the more resources you can bring to bear on a problem, the more likely you are to find a good solution.

And speaking of solutions, they are all there in the back of the book. Forget about our solution until you have finished the puzzle *your* way. A major reason for sticking with a puzzle until you have mastered it, painful as it may be, is that it benefits you in the same way "no pain, no gain" does in a physical exercise routine. It builds up the same kind of stamina. It's known as "concentration" in mental performance. Perseverance can be improved in the same way that aerobic training equips you to run or swim longer and longer each time. Often, superior concentration powers will win a competitive race to a solution.

A few housekeeping points:

We first created most of the puzzle formats in this book of mental exercises for a daily column requested by *The New York Times* to syndicate outside the United States in the 1980s. We called it "Playspace" and meant it. Play is an essential activity to further learning. Consider the most ferociously productive period of learning in your own life. Between the ages of two and six you taught yourself the grammar and vocabulary of a language you had never heard before. You learned the rules of right and wrong in a confused society. You stood up, risked gravity and walked forward. You moved from convenience to duty when you bought into potty training. That's a lot to accomplish in four years. The whole time you were playing, or so it seemed to all those huge people around you who were busy doing important things with their lives. You were really studying them like laboratory animals that fed *you*, picking up clues as fast as your neurons could scamper. Long live a light and eager heart!

For most of our mature lives, David and I have been joyfully engaged in learning how the human brain works its miracles — and devising tasks for it. We hope we have chosen well enough to captivate your interest and entertain your neurons while they stretch.

— Allen Bragdon, Cape Cod, April 2001

Section One
EXECUTIVE

The *Executive Function* in the human brain is located in the frontal part of the forehead above the eyes. This area has evolved after the other areas of the primate brain. It is also the last to mature in children and does not fully develop until after the age of nine. Some neurophysiologists even claim it is not fully developed until the early 20's — a view also held by many parents based on their empirical evidence. As in the L.I.F.O. (Last In, First Out) system of inventory management, its accumulated bundle of human skills tends to be the first to deteriorate with age.

Executive thinking tools are comprised of cleverly-designed devices. One such devise is *Working Memory* which holds data in mind temporarily while the brain manipulates it. Notice, for example, how you multiply 89 x 91 in your head. Or read the following sentence and answer the question that appears on the next page. "The waitress asked the busboy to clear the blue dishes but leave the bread basket for the bartender to take home to his parrot."

Business executives are, or should be, skilled at visualizing possible future paths for the firm and charting the intermediate steps required to achieve the chosen goal. As new data emerges, the executive must adapt original strategies without sacrificing the goal.

Accordingly, Executive functions include the capacity to alter responses to adjust to new data. The brain can adapt responses productively as the patterns of incoming data change, while still keeping the original goal in mind. *Einstellung* is the German word used by neuropsychologists to identify a mind set that cannot spot a new trend in a stream of data. Those minds continue to respond in an unproductive manner.

Many of the mental exercises in this section utilize *convergent* logic skills in which the working memory examines the data presented and works out the only correct conclusion. (Data: *Socrates is a man. All men are mortal.* Conclusion: *Socrates is mortal.*)

Divergent Intelligence, on the other hand, equips the mind to spot unfamiliar patterns. Often, they are newly forming within familiar data. It is also processed in the prefrontal area where Executive functions reside. In many senses it is the anthesis of the *Einstellung* mind set. Interestingly, if the frontal area of the brain is damaged, convergent thinking skills are lost but the IQ remains unchanged. On page 190, you will find a game to play with someone else that reveals tendencies to think either inside or outside the envelope, or both. (Who wanted the bread basket?)

As the brain ages, the ability to manipulate data quickly with the Working Memory tool slows down. In fact it begins losing its edge when the brain has become fully mature in the early 20's. The rate of loss stays constant into old age but the cumulative effect commonly does not show up until "senior moments" begin to occur in the 60's.

The good news is that most Executive function skills can be maintained by using them — working on the mental exercises in this book, for example. Because this galaxy of skills is essential to the highest levels of thinking, of insight and of productive behavior, they are worth cultivating lifelong to maintain the highest quality of life.

DIRECTIONS

Each symbol represents a digit, and always the same digit. Two symbols denote a two-digit number. How long will it take you to decode this puzzle?

Didjaknow...   **"EXECUTIVE" IS AMONG THE MOST RECENTLY-EVOLVED FUNCTIONS**

The Executive functions which evolved in the most anterior (forward) part of the human brain just above the eyebrow, perform the most uniquely human cognitive tasks. These include planning behavior and control of instinctive responses to achieve goals set for the future. The Executive function interprets current data for its value in time-future. It also coordinates sophisticated physical movements such as those needed to speak words. Prefrontal skills are located in two areas of the brain: *Prefrontal cortex*, the outer surface of the front sides, and *orbital frontal* regions, from the front center point deep down to the brain's interior. There, it links with the more primitive, *limbic* systems including the *hippocampus* (helps route data into memory) and *amygdala* (keeps alert for crucial new data).

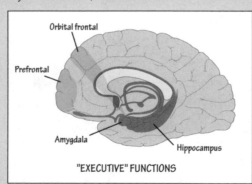

Orbital frontal

Prefrontal

Amygdala

Hippocampus

"EXECUTIVE" FUNCTIONS

Answer on page 211

& + [+ * = ! (

$ + ¢ + * = ! (

+ ¢ + [= ! (

% + * + [+ (= ! (

! + ¢ + % + * = ! (

% + & + * + $ = ! (

¢ + $ + % + # = ! (

The Angry*!$%?Typist

DIRECTIONS

Each symbol represents a digit, and always the same digit. Double symbols represent two-digit numbers. The asterisk represents an arithmetical sign, but not necessarily the same sign in each equation. Try to figure out the values of the symbols. Yes, the answers are all the same number.

Didjaknow... HAVING TO DEAL WITH UNFAMILIAR DATA KEEPS BRAINS YOUNG

Interestingly, older university professors tested in Executive function skills, which include Working Memory tasks, score higher than people of the same age who have followed other walks of life. Their scores on such tests are more competitive with test scores of young graduate students. Coping with change such as new students each year, new discoveries in their chosen fields and changing administrative policies may be the causative factors.

Answer on page 211

		&	!	*	?	@	=	•	#
		"	*	@	*	?	=	•	#
		¢	*	¢	*	#	=	•	#
	"	*	¢	*	!	•	=	•	#
&	"	*	&	*	!	=	•	#	
(	(	*	!	¢	*	•	=	•	#

HINT: The exclamation point is a one and the question mark is a three.

Thirty-Four All

DIRECTIONS

Using all the numbers 5 through 16 only once, make a magic square in which the sum of the numbers you insert in the boxes will be the same horizontally, vertically, and along each diagonal. In this case 34 is the magic number.

Didjaknow... KEEPING BRAINS SHARP IN RETIREMENT

Moral: To stay sharp as you age, keep Executive Functions active by, for example, plotting out a garden with seasonal timing, or planning and preparing a dinner party suited to new guests. Even reorganizing that messy bedroom closet is a task that works physical and mental muscle. (Bonus point: Brain researchers find, over and over, that physical activity clearly maintains mental acuity.)

Answer on page 211

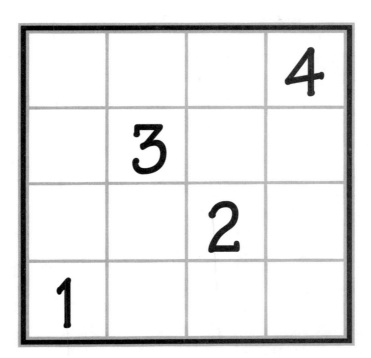

HINT: The numbers you insert in the two blank inside boxes should total 29.
The numbers in the two blank corner boxes should also total 29.

DIRECTIONS

In the box, opposite, each digit from 1 to 9 is used only once. The first and second row of digits are added to obtain the sum in the bottom row. Rearrange these digits in seven similar boxes so that the sum increases each time by 9. More than one solution is possible.

Didjaknow...

DIFFERENCES IN ABILITIES CAN BE OBSERVED IN INFANCY

Many sex differences can be documented shortly after birth. Females generally show a greater reaction to faces and are more sensitive to language sounds. Girls also tend to speak earlier and complete sentences earlier. Baby boys tend to get up, walk, and run earlier than girls. They also develop motor and spatial abilities earlier than girls.

Answer on page 211

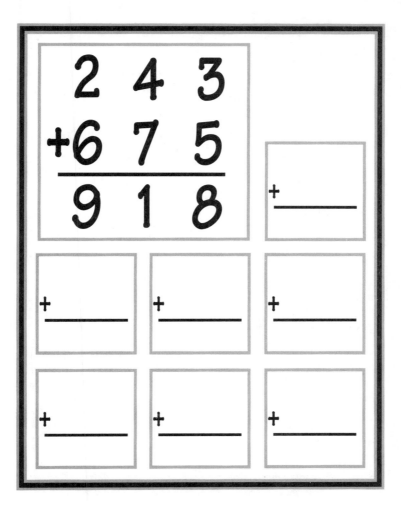

$$\begin{array}{r} 2\ 4\ 3 \\ +6\ 7\ 5 \\ \hline 9\ 1\ 8 \end{array}$$

+ _____

+ _____   + _____   + _____

+ _____   + _____   + _____

HINT: Adding 9 to each succeeding total leaves you with just 6 numbers to rearrange.

DIRECTIONS

Each horizontal row in the grid on the facing page has the same mathematical relationship. If you can identify the pattern, you will be able to supply the missing numbers in the bottom row.

Didjaknow...

INFANTS LIKE TO TAKE ACTION

Although a human needs to be at least six years of age to *imagine* the cause and effect of a sequence of events, an infant quickly learns to repeat a physical movement that produces an obvious reward. If a string is attached from an infant's toe to a visible mobile, an infant quickly catches on that each time he kicks his leg the mobile will move. This action will be repeated to the delight and fascination of the infant. To keep an infant occupied while you go about your duties, set him up with toys that provide a direct, physical connection between action and reward.

Answer on page 211

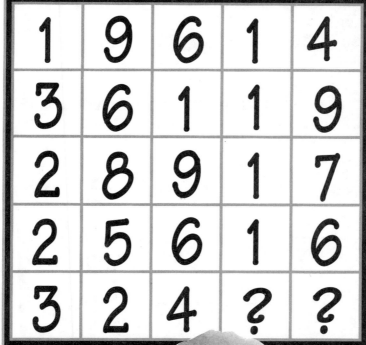

1	9	6	1	4
3	6	1	1	9
2	8	9	1	7
2	5	6	1	6
3	2	4	?	?

HINT: *Work horizontally row by row, first with the first three numbers, then with the last two.*

DIRECTIONS

The magic numbers for the wheel of fortune are: 34, 42, 43, 50, 51, 52, 59, 60, and 68. Place each of these numbers in the proper circle so that:

1. The three numbers on each straight line equal 153.
2. The numbers in circles ABC, CDE, EFG, and GHA also equal 153.

We have placed the number 59 in a circle to get you started.

Didjaknow... **ABILITY TESTS SHOW GENDER DIFFERENCES**

When a group of over a hundred men and women underwent a battery of neuropsychological function tests, sex differences immediately became apparent in some functions. The results showed that on tests of abstraction and mental flexibility, there was no significant difference between males and females. When it came to face memory and verbal memory, both immediate and delayed, women did significantly better than men. However, on tests of motor skill and spatial ability, men performed noticeably better than women.

Answer on page 211

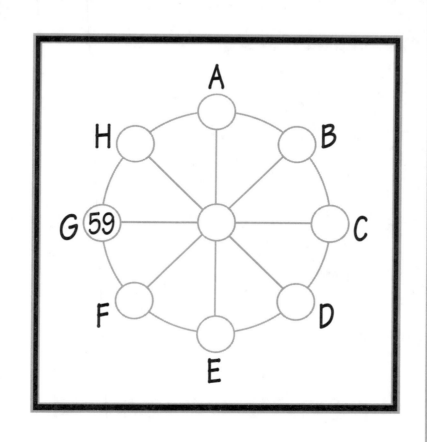

From Monday to Friday, Calvin diligently oversees the Department of Development and Plucking at Feathered Friends International. It's a demanding position which requires frequent business trips around FFI's far-flung poultry empire.

When the Accounting Department asked him to estimate how much time he spent on the road, Calvin referred to his fourth-quarter journal for a recent year. It revealed that in a six-week period he was in the office on the first of the month, then the 4th, 8th, 9th, 11th, 12th, 22nd, 25th, 28th, 29th, 30th, and the 4th and 8th of the following month.

Answer on page 211

During this period Calvin worked only one Saturday when he had to go in to supervise the de-feathering of an extremely hostile group of squabs.

Can you figure out which days of the week Calvin reported to his office during those six weeks? If you can, then you won't have any trouble discovering which months Calvin referred to in his journal.

Didjaknow... FEMALES AND MALES BOTH MENTALLY FLEXIBLE

Healthy humans of both sexes do equally well on abstraction and flexibility tests (ABF tests). ABF tests measure the ability to create concepts out of images or examples and the ability to shift previous concepts to new ones when the images are shifted. On a battery of tests, men and women were asked to guess the category by which to sort certain objects. As the category changed during testing, both sexes realized the category shifted and applied new principles to the sorting task. Difficulties in ABF, however, can occur in either sex if there is damage sustained to the front part of the brain called the frontal lobe.

HINT: Sketch a seven-day calendar grid for six weeks and fill in the blanks.

DIRECTIONS

Convert these eight domino equations to numbers. A domino placed vertically denotes a fraction or division. If the domino is placed horizontally, the pips are added. One horizontal domino above another also signifies a fraction or division of the total number of pips. A blank is zero.

Didjaknow... THE MALE BRAIN AGES FASTER

When compared with women, men not only have a proportionately higher percent of white matter in their brain, they also have more fluid in their brain. Every time a brain cell dies it is replaced with cerebrospinal fluid. The amount of fluid in the brain indicates brain atrophy or death of brain cells. Anatomically, as men age, they loose brain tissue at about three times the rate of women. As for actual brain function, men between the ages of 18 and 45 increasingly lose their capacity to pay attention effectively on all ability tests, but especially those involving verbal memory. Women did not show any decline in this age group.

Answer on page 211

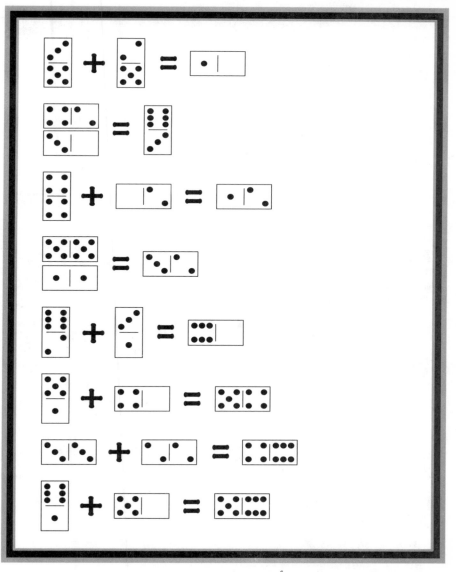

HINT: A whole number divided by 1 remains the same.

DIRECTIONS

Two ladies with three-letter first names are hiding in this maze of letters. See how many times you can spell out each of their names reading right to left, left to right, top to bottom, bottom to top, and both ways diagonally.

Didjaknow...

LEARNING IS HINDERED WHEN THE BRAIN CAN'T SAY "NO"

The deficits of attention deficit hyperactivity disorder (ADHD) are associated more with faulty output functions of the brain than the brain's intake functions. Recent research indicates that ADHD is not so much an "attention" disorder as an inhibition that leads to *intentional* disorder; the child's consciousness cannot filter out random data that is unproductive, so it acts on everything. Inhibition is often in conflict with intention, and an essential component of the brain's Executive Function is to just say "no" to unproductive impulses that interfere with achieving a desired goal. If the brain is not able to shut off impulses, negative consequences often result: intake, learning, and goals may not be attained.

Answer on page 211

The Able Accountant

Tom and Dick, their cousin Harry, and Jim the greengrocer have shared an accountant, Able, for the past few months. They are pleased with his work and are planning to surprise him with a salary increase at the end of four months, but can't agree when that would be. The discussion is taking place on the weekend — away from the stores where their records are kept. It goes as follows:

Tom: Able came to us at the end of December or the first of January.

Dick: My recollection is of a heavy snowstorm the week he started and I know we sold 15 snow throwers the first week in February.

Answer on page 212

Harry: No. We hired him quite a while after I opened my drug and vitamin business, which I think was about January 12th. He might have started in March.

Jim: His four months will be up in May or June.

Which statement could be correct?

Didjaknow... STRESS HORMONES MIGHT HELP OR MIGHT HURT

People would not survive without the production of the stress hormone adrenaline or cortisol. These hormones give humans the ability to react and respond. They essentially provide protection and adaptation in relation to life events. When people are new at public speaking, they often experience an increase in adrenaline and cortisol, and in turn, blood pressure and heart rate increases. After several speeches, adrenaline continues to rise, which is needed to give a speaker "the edge," but cortisol levels usually do not.
Cortisol affects almost all body functions: it has a direct influence on the receptors in a cell's nucleus, regulates metabolism in the liver and aspects of brain function, and affects the immune system, cardiovascular function, heart rate, and blood pressure. While stress hormones are needed for survival, prolonged increases of cortisol can have a negative influence and accelerate certain disease processes.

HINT: Who's guessing and who isn't?

DIRECTIONS

Opposite are two rows of three numbers each. Can you figure out the logical sequence of these numbers and fill in the final box in the third row?

Didjaknow... RAPID RESPONSE TO STROKE CAN SAVE YOUR LIFE

Strokes occur when blood flow to brain cells is blocked, frequently due to a clot in a blood vessel of the brain (ischemic stroke) or, less often, by hemorrhage of a vessel. In minutes, brain cells die and brain damage begins. Fortunately, there is a drug treatment called T.P.A. (tissue plasminogen activator) that can break up a clot, but it must be administered within three hours of the onset of a stroke. Symptoms of stroke include numbness or weakness on one side of the body, confusion or trouble speaking, sudden vision problems, dizziness or loss of balance, or severe unexplained headache. If you suspect an impending stroke, you only have a short time to act. Do not delay. Call 911 immediately so treatment can begin.

Answer on page 212

A	B	C
108	356	124
196	780	292
284	648	

HINT: Work horizontally. Do something to A and B to find a relationship with C.

Fives Are Wild

DIRECTIONS

Divide the 5 x 5 grid, opposite, into five sections of five squares each with no two digits alike, and the sum of the squares in each section having the same numerical value.

Didjaknow... THINKING INCREASES BLOOD FLOW TO THE BRAIN

For years, scientists thought blood flow to the brain was constant, but recent studies prove that blood flow increases when you think. In order to think, the brain has to create energy. Energy is created by breaking down glucose, and to do that, fresh oxygen is needed from the blood. After glucose is broken down, byproducts of metabolism are released and quickly taken up by the blood and away from the brain. The body knows exactly what parts of the brain require extra blood. Blood flow will increase to the area specialized for the problem being solved. PET scan studies show blood flow increases more in the left brain for analogies and more in the right brain for tests that require spatial reasoning.

Answer on page 212

3	9	4	7	8
8	1	5	2	3
7	8	3	6	5
6	5	7	4	1
4	3	2	5	9

HINT: The sum of the squares in each section is 25.

DIRECTIONS

Rearrange the figures in the squares, opposite, in such a way that each horizontal and vertical row and the two corner-to-corner diagonals total the sum of 30.

Didjaknow... **KNOWLEDGE OF THE WORLD INCREASES WITH AGE**

Although the brain's processing efficiency continuously declines with age, factual knowledge and experience do not. During the lifespan of an individual, knowledge gained through life experience increases rather than decreases with age. Thus, older individuals have the edge when it comes to experience, conceptual knowledge, judgment, and wisdom since only a lifetime of living can deliver such things. Throughout

history and across cultures around the world, young people rely on the wisdom of older adults. Even in today's American workplace, whether it be a law office, accounting firm, or the halls of academia, young adults gather and learn new data under the direction and instruction of older, more experienced adults.

Answer on page 212

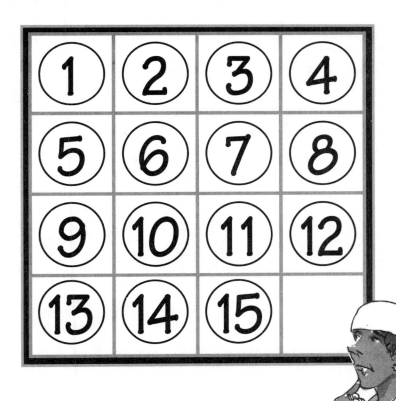

DIRECTIONS

If you've ever counted stars at night, here's a star-stumper to keep you busy. Twenty stars have been placed in the white squares, opposite, two stars in each horizontal and each vertical row. Can you place 20 more stars in the remaining empty squares? The catch: Only four stars are allowed in each horizontal and vertical row.

Didjaknow... MEN "FIGHT OR FLEE"; WOMEN "TEND AND BEFRIEND"

Studies on male rats indicate that crowding increases stress because it elevates the stress hormone cortisol. With female rats, the reverse effect occurs: crowding appears to calm them. In humans, men tend to seek seclusion on arriving home from work and prefer to be left alone. If men have been under stress all day at work, they are more likely to provoke conflict within the family. In contrast, women under work-related stress, upon returning home, are more likely to cope by concentrating on their children. Studies show that even when women are under attack, they are more likely to protect their children and seek help from other females rather than fight and take flight.

Answer on page 212

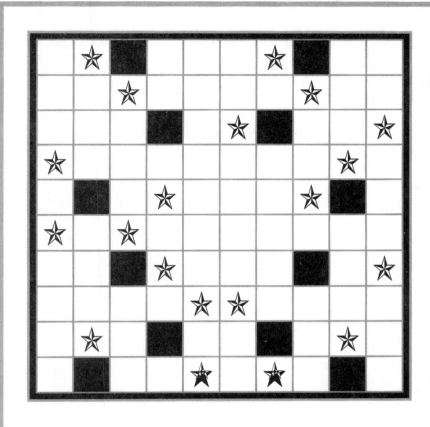

HINT: The four stars in the bottom row will stand side-by-side.

CITATIONS

P. 14 Gazzaniga, M. et al. (1998). Cognitive Neuroscience, W.W. Norton, New York.

P. 16, 18 Shimamura, A. et al. (1995). Memory and cognitive ability in university professors: evidence for successful aging. Psychological Science 6/5:271-7.

P. 20 Gur, Ruben C. Sex Differences in Learning. Using Brain Research to Reshape Classroom Practice. Public Information Resources, Inc. 7-9 Nov. 1999.

P. 22 Diamond, Adele. "Learning and the Brain" Conference. (1999) Boston, MA.

P. 24, 27, 28 Gur, Ruben C.

P. 30 Denckla, Martha Bridge, MD, Director, Developmental Cognitive Neurology, The Johns Hopkins School of Medicine. From a presentation at Science of Cognition Conference, Library of Congress, Washington, D.C., 6 Oct. 1999.

P. 33 McEwen, Bruce PhD, Head of Hatch Laboratory of Neuroendocrinology, Rockefeller University. From a presentation at Science of Cognition Conference, Library of Congress, Washington, D.C., 6 Oct. 1999.

P. 34 Cheresh, David, et al, Scripps Research Institute and others at Henry Ford Health Sciences Center, "Nature Medicine" (2001).

P. 36 Gur, Ruben C.

P. 38 Park, Denise PhD. The Center for Applied Cognitive Research on Aging, University of Michigan. From a presentation at the Science of Cognition Conference. Library of Congress, Washington, D.C., 6 Oct. 1999.

P. 40 S.E. Taylor et al. (2000). Biobehavioral Responses to Stress in Females: Tend-and-Befriend, Not Fight-or-Flight. Psychological Review 107/3: 411-29.

Section Two
MEMORY

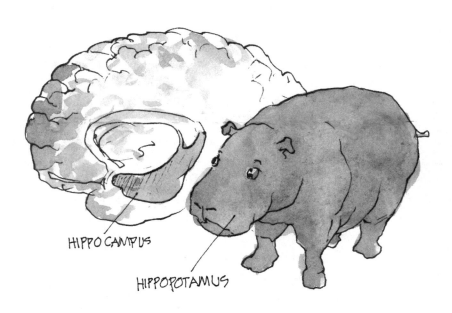

HIPPOCAMPUS

HIPPOPOTAMUS

T his is about memory(s), plural, because the brain uses many different strategies to store data, retrieve it and distort it. If you know something about how these systems work you can tap the brain's built-in memory systems strategies to devise the best strategy each time.

Explicit memory (sometimes called *declarative* memory) is the kind you use when you consciously make an effort to remember something. Your brain stores *implicit, nondeclarative,* memories without your even knowing it has happened, much less being aware of trying. That is how you learned your native language, for example.

Here are two strategies for converting new data into long term explicit memory. Repeat the data in different ways: write it down, say it aloud, explain it to someone else, diagram it. Let it rest a while, then go over it again. Spacing out those rehearsal sessions will help.

Another method of learning new data is to steal a trick from your implicit memory system. Your implicit memory of an event (called *episodic* memory) becomes permanent because it was emotionally charged — your wedding day, an accident or the name of your first lover, for example. Often you can artificially apply an emotional "tag" to otherwise dull facts by associating them with some other weird or dramatic memory.

Relate all new data to existing memories. The more familiar hooks you hang a new fact on the more likely you will be able to recall it. Why? Your memory of something that happened to you is stored in many different parts of your brain. The smells of it in one place, the colors, the touch sensations, the sounds of it all in different arrays of cells. When you recall it, any one of those components can trigger the brain to go around and collect all the others to reconstruct the richness of the whole event. When you try to commit a description of an "event" to memory, say a date in history or a list of criteria for a diagnosis, create as many possible "triggers" as you can by visualizing the "event" in association with many different senses and familiar places or other events.

Strategies are important if you want to improve memory skills because practice does not help. Where practice does help is to lengthen the time you can concentrate on a task, much as you can build lung capacity, then stamina, with aerobic exercise. The short answer to building up the ability to focus longer is to force yourself to stay with a task. So don't put down the puzzle the first time you hit a wall working it. Pause, if you like, to think a minute, but don't quit. If you are stuck, look at the hint printed upside down to get going again. Every time you don't quit you build the capacity to stick with it longer, if only a little. The effect is cumulative and worth the effort. If you can't concentrate you can't develop the *explicit* memory strategies you will need to enter new data into memory.

Beware of false memory. True memory can easily become distorted when you recall it. The brain organizes the vast store of data it must recall by piecing it back together in ways that follow other past experience. When details are missing, it tries to insert what "must" have happened. It will also fill in details that are suggested to it by the way a question is posed when you are asked to recall something.

Why you forget also reveals something about why you remember. When two bunches of data command your attention in sequence, such as when you read two stories in an anthology, your memory of details of the first will dim for a while, a natural occurrence called *retroactive inhibition*. That is why people sometimes find themselves in a place but can't recall what they went there for. Usually it is because something interesting commanded their attention on the way there.

The Early Early Bird

ENTRY LEVEL

Natalie Nuthatch knew she'd have the pick of the crop at local yard sales if she arrived early enough, but on this particular Saturday morning she arrived before the setting-up preparations had been completed. Asked to come back at the appointed hour, a chastened Natalie made a surreptitious inventory of the items already on display before beating a retreat and, upon returning at the proper time, quickly noted the items that had been added during her absence. Study the array of objects that Natalie first observed in the top picture, then turn the page upside-down and examine the objects in the lower picture that she found upon her return. Without looking back at the first picture, can you tell which items had been added to the sale?

Didjaknow... MEMORY IS THE MOTHER OF ALL FUNCTIONS

When anything goes wrong with the brain, the first system affected is memory. Any fluctuation in mental state, such as depression, anxiety, or stress, will have a negative impact on the brain's memory system. Following a brain injury, memory is almost always the first thing that goes. Damage to the parietal and temporal parts on the left side of the brain is most likely to affect language memory since the left hemisphere specializes in language, verbal, and analytic processes. The right hemisphere specializes in spatial, facial, more Gestalt processes; damage to this side is more likely to affect spatial reasoning and spatial memory.

Answer on page 212

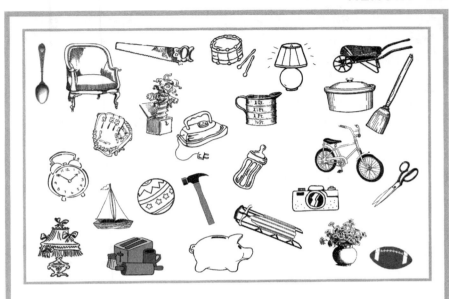

Lucky Thirteen

DIRECTIONS

Your goal is to go from 13 to 181 in 10 moves, performing the arithmetical function to the digit in the square selected as you proceed. You may start from either corner but — and here's the trick — only one corner is correct. Moves may be made horizontally and vertically, but not diagonally.

Didjaknow... YOUNG BRAINS AND OLD BRAINS DECLINE AT THE SAME RATE

Old brains DON'T decline more rapidly; they just begin to show it. A large sample of adults, between the ages of 20 to 90, underwent a battery of tests for working memory and overall mental function. The tests revealed how much information they could remember, manipulate, and retrieve. Interestingly, results revealed that brain decline begins when people are in their 20's and continues at the same pace across their entire lifespan. Therefore, a 60- or 70-year-old brain is not actually declining any more rapidly than a 30-year-old's. Although the decline begins in young adulthood, the cumulative effects on brain function do not show up in behavior until adults grow much older.

Answer on page 212

13	³ X	⁴ −	⁴ X	⁵ +	⁴ X	**13**
⁷ X	⁴¹ −	² ÷	⁷ +	³ ÷	¹¹ +	⁸ X
¹⁴ +	⁶ ÷	² X	⁴ −	¹⁷ X	⁴ ÷	³ +
⁵ ÷	³³ −	⁵ ÷	⁷ +	⁸ ÷	⁶ X	⁴¹ −
²¹ X	¹²³ +	⁸ −	¹⁴ ÷	² −	³ ÷	⁷¹ X
¹⁴ −	⁶ −	¹² +	⁹³ X	⁴ +	⁷² −	¹⁰ ÷
= 181	= 181	= 181	= 181	= 181	= 181	= 181

HINT: Aim for the 181 that's second from the left in the bottom row.

Great Scott!

DIRECTIONS

The answers to the clues are names. Choose a letter that appears at least once anywhere in the full name. The correct letter must appear as many times in the name as the available number of boxes allotted for its clue number, reading *across* only. (For example, if clue #9 were "Bjorn Borg" you could try either B's, O's, or R's in the two squares allotted.) When correctly chosen, each row across will repeat the same letter. Every column will spell out the theme-word for this puzzle. For sports fans this one may be "Entry Level."

CLUES

1. Spanish golfing great
2. Boxing great (né)
3. Brazilian soccer great
4. New York Islanders great
5. Auto racing great
6. LPGA great
7. Chicago Bears great
8. U.S. Olympic swimming great
9. Swedish tennis great
10. Australian tennis great
11. Jockey great
12. Montreal Canadiens great
13. Cleveland Browns great
14. Boston Red Sox great
15. Kansas City Royals great
16. German figure skating great
17. Detroit Lions great
18. Chess great

Answer on page 212

1			2		
3	4	5	6	7	8
9		10			
11		12			13
14	15		16		
17		18			

Didjaknow... OLD BRAINS USE MORE BRAIN

When researchers asked young and old subjects to do a certain verbal working memory task, the young adults used only their left frontal cortex; older ones also used areas elsewhere in both their left and right hemispheres. On another test young adults needed only a few specialized brain circuits but, again, older adults had to use more of their brain to perform the same task. The aging brain may recruit underused healthy circuits when the circuits originally specialized for a certain task begin to fail.

HINT: We already gave you one.

DIRECTIONS

The answers to the clues are names. Choose a letter that appears at least once anywhere in the full name. The correct letter must appear as many times in the name as the available number of boxes allotted for each clue number, reading *across* only. (For example, #2 needs the first letters of her first and last names to fill its two boxes.) When correctly chosen, each row across will repeat the same letter. Each column will repeat the theme-word appropriate to this puzzle.

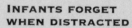

Didjaknow... INFANTS FORGET WHEN DISTRACTED

An infant will reach for a reward placed under a cup, but if she sees you move it under another cup, and you distract her, she will look for it under the first cup. Because the brain has not matured enough to hold the new data, it only takes four seconds of diversion for the infant to forget the second action and revert to the first. Until language skills are acquired, the same forgetful response occurs in children two years of age or older when distraction is long-lasting between replacing the reward and reaching for it. For parents this can be a plus: next time your infant wants to grab a hazardous object, distract the infant by replacing the undesirable object with one that is safe.

Answer on page 212

1	2		3	
4				5
6			7	
8				9
10			11	

CLUES

1. Television and nightclub comedienne
2. Singer and movie actress
3. "Taxi" sit-com star
4. Hollywood's Butch Cassidy
5. New Orleans trumpeter
6. The "greatest" prizefighter
7. 1975 Wimbledon winner
8. Three baseball brothers
9. Early television comedian
10. Doyenne of the whodunit
11. Lucy's love

HINT: #5 is Al Hirt. Note that #8 includes the full names of all three brothers.

Heavenly Harmonies

DIRECTIONS

The answers to the clues are names. Choose a letter that appears at least once anywhere in the full name. The correct letter must appear as many times in the name as the available number of boxes allotted for each clue number, reading *across* only. (For example, the correct name for #13 would allow either two A's or two H's.) When correctly chosen, each row across will repeat the same letter. Every column will spell out the same theme-word appropriate to this puzzle.

CLUES

1. Jazz trumpeter (1926-1991)
2. *South Pacific* star (1913-1990)
3. American dancer and choreographer (1894-1991)
4. Jazz pianist (1920-1982)
5. Austrian composer (1797-1828)
6. French composer (1862-1918)
7. Austrian waltz composer (1825- 1899)
8. American composer (1896-1985)
9. Violin superstar (1901-1987)
10. *West Side Story* composer (1918-1990)
11. *William Tell* composer (1792-1868)
12. Opera superstar (1873-1921)
13. "Stardust" composer (1899-1981)
14. *Appalachian Spring* composer (1900-1990)

Answer on page 213

1	2		3	
4	5	6		7
8				9
10	11			
12		13		14

Didjaknow...

MORE BRAIN, MORE MEMORY GAINED

The more the brain encodes, the better the memory. Subjects were given memorizing tasks: lists of words; sets of unfamiliar faces; and sets of nameable pictures such as a line-drawn dog. The brain's left dorsal frontal region memorizes word lists (verbal), while unfamiliar faces require the right prefrontal brain (nonverbal). Because nameable pictures use both sides of the brain (two codes), they were remembered best.

HINT: #13 is Hoagy Carmichael.

DIRECTIONS

Solve this puzzle as you would a crossword puzzle using numbers instead of words. Only the digits 1 through 9 are used; there are no zeros. Only one digit may be placed in each box, and a digit may be used more than once in an answer. Where it appears that more than one combination of digits is possible, look for additional clues in the interlocking answers. A prime number is divisible only by itself and 1.

CLUES

ACROSS

1. The beginning of the French Revolution
4. A prime number
5. The Arabic number denoting which Louis was in power at the time of 1 Across
7. 17—, the execution of Revolutionary leader Georges Danton
8. 17—, the birth of painter Corot
9. The month and day in 1793 of the execution of 5 Across; the square of a prime number
10. Birth year of painter Delacroix

DOWN

1. The end of the French Revolution; birth year of novelist Balzac
2. Bastille Day (month and day)
3. An odd number; the sum of the second and fourth digits is one-third of each of the other digits
6. An even number; each of the first two digits is three less than the sum of the last two digits
9. A prime number that is also the reverse of 4 Across

Answer on page 213

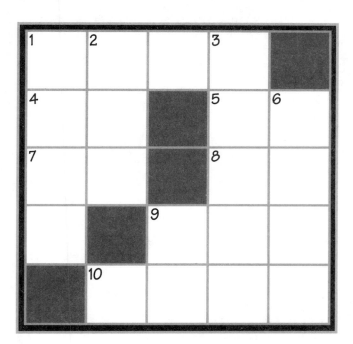

Didjaknow...   LONG TERM STRESS HURTS THE HIPPO (AND MEMORY)

Long-term stress can harm a part of the brain called the hippocampus. The hippocampus contains receptors for the stress hormone cortisol and repeated increases of cortisol can impair declarative memory. The hippocampus can withstand short-term stress, but if stress is long-term, results are more negative. The hippocampus in people with recurrent depressive illness becomes 10-12 percent smaller in volume.

HINT: The sum of 9 Across is 4.

DIRECTIONS

Solve this puzzle as you would a crossword puzzle using numbers instead of words. Only the digits 1 through 9 are used; there are no zeros. Only one digit may be placed in each box, and a digit may be used more than once in an answer. Where it appears that more than one combination of digits is possible, look for additional clues in the interlocking answers. A prime number is divisible only by itself and 1.

CLUES

ACROSS

1. The month and day of a patriotic observance
3. The year Congress adopted the Stars and Stripes
5. Each digit increases by 2
7. When viewed as double-digit numbers, the first two digits are half as great as the last two
8. The cube of a prime number

DOWN

1. The sum of the digits is 25
2. The year of American Independence
3. A prime number
4. The sum of the digits is 17
6. See 4 Down

Answer on page 213

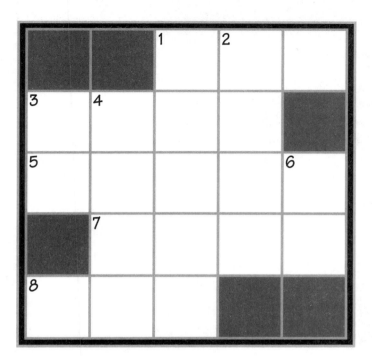

Didjaknow... MUSICAL TRAINING IMPROVES MEMORY

Studies show adults who received musical training before the age of 12 have a 16% better memory for the spoken word than other adults. Brain circuits exercised while performing music are used in many other mental abilities, so young children who pick up music will have stronger skills and capacities later in life.

HINT: Flag Day is June 14th.

Birth of a Nation

DIRECTIONS

Solve this puzzle as you would a crossword puzzle using numbers instead of words. Only the digits 1 through 9 are used; there are no zeros. Only one digit may be placed in each box, and a digit may be used more than once in an answer. Where it appears that more than one combination of digits is possible, look for additional clues in the interlocking answers. A prime number is divisible only by itself and 1.

CLUES

ACROSS

1. The month and day of a national holiday
3. A bad luck number
5. The year celebrated in 1 Across
7. A prime number, followed by its square and cube
8. The bicentennial anniversary of 5 Across
10. A good luck number

DOWN

2. The sum of its digits is 16
3. The first anniversary of 5 Across
4. A square
6. Well-known Boeing number plus 2
9. A square

Answer on page 213

Didjaknow... WOMEN ARE BETTER AT VERBAL MEMORY

In both immediate and delayed verbal memory, women outperform men. When asked to memorize a list of 16 items, most women knew the list on the second repetition, while it took men five tries. After a new "interference" list was given as a distraction, subjects were later asked to recite the first list. Again, women scored higher than the men on average.

HINT: *Independence Day.*

DIRECTIONS

Next to each of the 20 letters, opposite, there is a group of seven numbers. How many groups can you find that are composed of the same seven numbers, although not necessarily in the same order?

Didjaknow... EARLY TO BED MAKES YOU WISE

The college practice of cramming until dawn may lead to failure rather than success. Researchers find that, for most people, 6 to 8 hours of sleep is needed for optimal learning of new information. Particularly important are the first 2 hours of sleep, called slow-wave sleep, and the final 2 hours of sleep, called REM or dream sleep. During these sleep phases, the brain sorts, files, and stores data so it can be retrieved when needed. College students looking to make the dean's list might want to close their books and head to bed early the night before an exam.

Answer on page 213

a	2 6 1 0 4 1 7
b	8 3 7 1 9 4 5
c	1 8 3 1 5 2 7
d	5 7 0 1 2 5 8
e	1 2 3 2 4 3 1
f	8 1 4 9 5 3 7
g	9 2 3 1 3 4 9
h	1 5 8 4 8 6 8
i	5 3 7 9 8 1 4
j	7 3 1 3 2 5 0

k	1 6 0 3 5 3 6
l	2 7 1 7 4 6 9
m	4 1 7 3 9 5 8
n	3 6 9 1 6 2 1
o	1 8 2 7 7 7 5
p	3 0 1 0 5 1 2
q	2 1 9 4 9 8 4
r	5 3 7 1 9 4 8
s	1 6 8 3 8 9 0
t	4 0 2 1 5 0 3

HINT: There are five groups with the same numbers.

Circles Within Circles

DIRECTIONS

This exercise works your brain in circles. The heavily circled number 1 is surrounded by six other numbers — all different. Search the vase for nine additional similar combinations: a number surrounded by six other numbers, none of which is alike.

Didjaknow... THE SOUND OF LANGUAGE IS IMPORTANT FOR COMPREHENSION

The brain uses special tricks to discriminate and translate fast-moving spoken syllables into meaningful words and to convert patterns of letters on a printed page into meaningful spoken words. In both cases, the ability to hold sounds in short-term "working" memory is crucial.

To understand the meaning of any sentence, the brain must hold in memory the idea started by the words in the first part of the sentence while the eyes or ears are taking in the words in the last part of the sentence — just as you did when you read this one. If a child who is learning to read, can also hear the words in his "mind's ear," he can hold in memory the sound of the beginning of the sentence long enough to add meaning to what the second half of the sentence expresses.

Answer on page 213

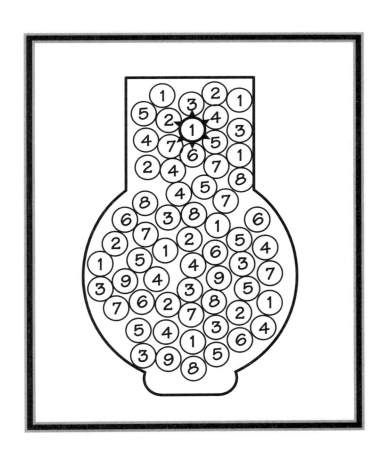

CITATIONS

P. 46 Gur, Ruben C. PhD. Sex Differences in Learning. Using Brain Research to Reshape Classroom Practice. From a presentation at the Learning and the Brain Conference. Boston, MA, 7-9 Nov. 1999.

P. 48 Park, Denise PhD. The Center for Applied Cognitive Research on Aging, University of Michigan. From a presentation at the Science of Cognition Conference. Library of Congress, Washington, D.C., 6 Oct. 1999.

P. 51 Park, Denise PhD.

P. 52 Diamond, Adele. "Learning and the Brain" Conference. Boston, MA, 7-9 Nov. 1999.

P. 55 Petersen, Steven E. PhD. Department of Neurology and Neurological Surgery, Washington University School of Medicine. From a presentation at Science of Cognition Conference, Library of Congress, Washington, D.C., 6 Oct. 1999.

P. 57 McEwen, Bruce PhD., Head of the Hatch Laboratory of Neuroendocrinology, Rockefeller University. From a presentation at Science of Cognition Conference, Library of Congress, Washington, D.C., 6 Oct. 1999.

P. 59 Chen, Agnes S., Yim-Chi Ho, and Mei-Chun Cheung (1998). Nature 396:128.

P. 61 Gur, Ruben C. PhD.

P. 62 Stickgold, R. et al. (2000). Visual discrimination task improvement: a multi-step process occurring during sleep. Journal of Cognitive Neuroscience 12/2:246-54.

P. 64 Eden, Guinevere D.Phil., Georgetown University Medical Center. From a presentation at Science of Cognition Conference, Library of Congress, Washington, D.C., 6 Oct. 1999.

Section Three
COMPUTATION

What part of your brain will you be exercising as you work on the tasks in the Computation Section? Many researchers believe there are different information-processing styles associated with each of your brain's hemispheres. The left is analytic, linear, serial-processing; it sees every tree in the forest, laboriously analyzing and inspecting each in turn. The right is synthetic, simultaneous, parallel-processing; it quickly sizes up the shape and texture of the forest as a whole.

Language and math may seem to be strictly linear, hence left-brain, skills. Both manipulate units of sound and sight (phonemes, syllables, digits and symbols) that can be combined in many ways according to rules. However, complex problem-solving skills like those must draw on systems in both hemispheres. For example, the flash of insight that led Einstein to his theory of relativity occurred as he considered the moving hands of the town-hall clock through the window of the moving tram on the way to work. That time-space insight was right-brain. The painstaking process of translating that insight into numbers was left-brain.

Two of the puzzle formats in this section are a lot like crossword puzzles with numbers rather than words. The interlocking answers to the clues help eliminate incorrect responses. The strategy is to fill in obvious answers as extra clues to pare down possibilities for the others. Take a look at the simplified fragment on the facing page, for example. If you look at each clue in turn, you'll see that every one suggests multiple solutions. Any line of boxes, taken alone, could be filled in with any of several answers, but only some of those answers could be compatible with the clues given for intersecting lines of boxes.

Clues: 1 Across   13 x 1, 2, or 3

3 Across   A palindrome; the
first digit is the
square root of the
last two

2 Down   A square

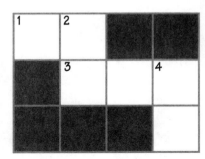

For example, 1 Across could be 13, 26, or 39 and 2 Down could be 16, 25, 36, 49, 64, or 81. But since the second digit of 1 Across is also the first digit of 2 Down, the latter could only be 36 or 64.

So 3 Across must begin with 6 or 4. Let's say it begins with 6. Since the answer must be a palindrome (a number that reads the same forwards and backwards), and the first digit must be the square root of the last two, the answer could be 636. What about the other possibility? If 3 Across begins with 4, then the next two digits would have to be 16 by the square root requirement — but then, it wouldn't be a palindrome. So 3 Across must be 636, 2 Down must be 36, 1 Across must be 13.

To review a few terms: A "square" of any number (say 3) is the number you get when you multiply it by itself (9). The "square root" is the number you started with (3). A "cube" results from multiplying that answer again by itself (81). A "prime" number is any one that cannot be divided evenly except by 1 and itself (For example, 3 or 7 are , but not 6 or 21). "Digits" are the basic numbers in a system or set. In our decimal system they are 0 through 10; in binary system code they are 0 and 1. "Integers" are the numbers you say when you count. Have fun!

DIRECTIONS

Solve this puzzle as you would a crossword puzzle, using interlocking numbers instead of words. Write a single digit in each box so that the sum of the digits equals the total given for that row or column in the Across and Down clues. For example, the sum of the digits in the 1-Across boxes must total 13. No number is used more than once in any answer, and zero is not used. The digits already in place are correct, so use them as checkpoints to help get started.

Didjaknow... USE MATH, DON'T LOSE IT

While language skills tend to improve with age, the ability swiftly to perform complex number problems declines. Even expert mathematicians will experience this age-related decline in performance. However, it is possible to slow age-related declines in math performance by exercising math circuits. For example, work number puzzles, compose math equations to express a problem, estimate your checkbook balance in your head or add up the total cost of your grocery tab while waiting in the checkout line.

Answer on page 213

CLUES

ACROSS

1. 13
3. 13
5. 22
8. 8
10. 17
11. 15
12. 11
13. 12
15. 17
17. 13
18. 12

DOWN

2. 16
3. 15
4. 5
6. 16
7. 15
9. 13
10. 20
12. 9
14. 8
15. 14
16. 16

HINT: All the numbers in the rows and columns end with odd digits.

DIRECTIONS

Solve this puzzle as you would a crossword puzzle, using interlocking numbers instead of words. Write a single digit in each box so that the sum of the digits equals the total given for that row or column in the Across and Down clues. For example, the sum of the digits in the 1-Across boxes must total 34. No number is used more than once in any answer, and zero is not used. The digits already in place are correct.

CLUES

ACROSS

1. 34
5. 17
6. 11
8. 30
10. 16
11. 15
12. 28
14. 24
17. 20
18. 33

DOWN

1. 28
2. 21
3. 10
4. 17
5. 32
7. 31
9. 20
11. 28
13. 24
15. 11
16. 13

Didjaknow... COUNTING AND QUANTITY ARE TWO DIFFERENT CONCEPTS

Even though your child may be able to count to 10, this does not mean he understands that the number-word represents a quantity. Stack 9 blocks and ask your youngster to count them. Next, point to the stack and ask him how many blocks you placed in the stack. If he has to count again, he does not yet grasp the concept that the last number counted in a sequence signifies the quantity of the whole set.

Answer on page 213

	1	2	7	3	4	
5				6		7
8			9			6
10			7		11	
8			12	13		
14	15	16		17		
	18		7			

HINT: The digit 5 is never used in this puzzle.

Addendum & Eve?

DIRECTIONS

Solve this puzzle as you would a crossword puzzle, using interlocking numbers instead of words. Write a single digit in each box so that the sum of the digits equals the total given for that row or column in the Across and Down clues. For example, the sum of the digits in the 1-Across boxes must total 5. No number is used more than once in any answer, and zero is not used. Use the four correct digits already entered as checkpoints to help get started on the right foot.

Didjaknow... WHAT PARTS OF THE BRAIN LIGHT UP WHEN DOING MATH IN YOUR HEAD?

Simple math gets done in the *left angular gyrus* and the *medial parietal cortices* which process numerical representations during exact calculation and retrieve arithmetical facts from memory. More complex calculation tasks involving the application of rules, use the *left inferior frontal* areas, also used for language and for Working Memory (the kind used when say, multiplying 89 by 91 in your head, in which some data must be held in mind while other, but related, data is processed).

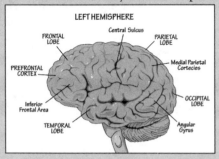

LEFT HEMISPHERE

Central Sulcus

FRONTAL LOBE

PARIETAL LOBE

Medial Parietal Cortecies

PREFRONTAL CORTEX

OCCIPITAL LOBE

Inferior Frontal Area

TEMPORAL LOBE

Angular Gyrus

Answer on page 214

■	1	2	■	3	4	■
5	■	6	7		■	8
9	10	■	**7**	■	11	
■	12	**4**		**6**		■
13		■	**6**	■	14	15
	■	16		17	■	
■	18		■	19		■

CLUES

ACROSS:

1. 5
3. 5
6. 23
9. 14
11. 17
12. 26
13. 15
14. 8
16. 18
18. 17
19. 12

DOWN

2. 12
3. 9
5. 13
7. 35
8. 15
10. 17
11. 23
13. 13
15. 10
16. 12
17. 14

HINT: *All the numbers in the rows and columns end with even digits.*

DIRECTIONS

Solve this puzzle as you would a crossword puzzle, using interlocking numbers instead of words. Write a single digit in each box so that the sum of the digits equals the total given for that row or column in the Across and Down clues. For example, the sum of the digits in the 1-Across boxes must total 35. No number is used more than once in any answer, and zero is not used. The entered numbers are correct.

CLUES

ACROSS		DOWN	
1. 35	13. 13	1. 20	9. 18
5. 15	15. 24	2. 26	12. 23
6. 20	17. 22	3. 17	14. 18
8. 30	19. 20	4. 24	16. 15
10. 12	20. 30	5. 34	18. 16
11. 20		7. 32	

Didjaknow... LEFT-BRAIN DAMAGE MAY INTERFERE WITH COMPUTATION

Left-brain damage can sometimes cause a condition referred to as *acalculia*. Patients suffering from acalculia are often able to give an answer to an easy, rote-memorized mathematical problem, such as 3 + 3 = 6. However, if the problem is complex and involves computation, such as 13 + 43, these patients will lack the ability to calculate and answer.

Answer on page 214

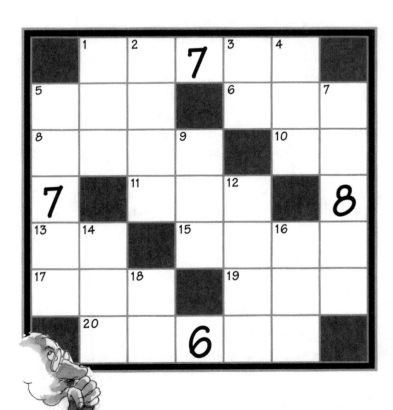

Tot Up & Tally Ho!

DIRECTIONS

Solve this puzzle as you would a crossword puzzle, using interlocking numbers instead of words. Write a single digit in each box so that the sum of the digits equals the total given for that row or column in the Across and Down clues. For example, the sum of the digits in the 1-Across boxes must total 30. No number is used more than once in any answer, and zero is not used. We have entered a few correct digits to get you started.

CLUES

ACROSS		DOWN	
1. 30	12. 20	1. 32	10. 10
6. 20	13. 15	2. 16	13. 23
7. 13	15. 15	3. 13	14. 19
8. 14	16. 15	4. 25	16. 15
9. 11	17. 29	5. 13	
11. 8		7. 18	

Didjaknow... NEWBORNS PERCEIVE DIFFERENCE IN QUANTITIES ONLY UP TO 3 OR 4

An infant seems to detect differences in numerical quantity. When a newborn is shown a picture of 3 dots, he becomes attentive. After repeatedly seeing the picture, he acts indifferent (habituates). Changing the number of dots arouses his interest again provided they range from 1-3 (sometimes 4). Newborns cannot discriminate differences above 3 or 4 so they do not respond. Those higher counts are too much for a newborn's brain to process until many months later in its development.

Answer on page 214

DIRECTIONS

Solve this puzzle as you would a crossword puzzle, using interlocking numbers instead of words. Write a single digit in each box so that the sum of the digits equals the total given for that row or column in the Across and Down clues. For example, the sum of the digits in the 1-Across boxes must total 18. No number is used more than once in any answer, and zero is not used. We have entered some correct digits as checkpoints.

CLUES

ACROSS

1. 18	15. 20
3. 19	16. 30
7. 13	18. 17
9. 22	19. 24
11. 13	21. 12
12. 28	24. 27
13. 25	25. 24
14. 20	

DOWN

1. 25	11. 33
2. 15	15. 26
4. 13	17. 23
5. 27	20. 15
6. 13	22. 14
8. 34	23. 16
9. 32	
10. 35	

Answer on page 214

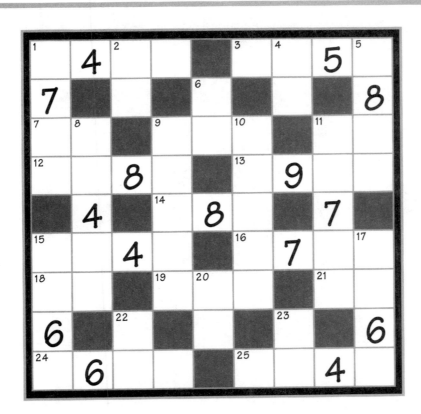

Didjaknow... A MYSTERIOUS AFFINITY FOR 7'S

The brain seems to put a limit on remembering a sequence of numbers at seven digits. Many systems are based on this limitation; days in the week, telephone numbers, and notes on the musical scale, for example.

HINT: 1 and 2 are not used.

DIRECTIONS

Solve this puzzle as you would a crossword puzzle, using interlocking numbers instead of words. Write a single digit in each box so that the sum of the digits equals the total given for that row or column in the Across and Down clues. For example, the sum of the digits in the 1-Across boxes must total 18. No number is used more than once in any answer, and zero is not used. The entered digits are correct.

CLUES

ACROSS		DOWN	
1. 18	17. 26	1. 18	16. 35
4. 8	19. 21	2. 35	18. 35
7. 11	21. 14	3. 23	20. 22
8. 22	23. 17	5. 16	22. 18
9. 17	25. 13	6. 29	24. 18
10. 23	26. 22	11. 24	
12. 12	27. 11	12. 20	
13. 39	28. 18	14. 13	
16. 26	29. 21	15. 21	

Didjaknow... JAPANESE WORDS FOR NUMBERS HELP THEM LEARN MATH EARLY

The Japanese learn to count earlier than English-speaking children, in part, because the names for numbers between 10 and 100 represent the numbers 1 through 9. For example, the number 10 is named "zyuu" and the number 2 is named "ni." The number-name for 12 is "zyuuni" or 10 + 2. Besides assisting with counting skills, the Japanese number-name system teaches the concept of quantity, making addition easier to grasp.

Answer on page 214

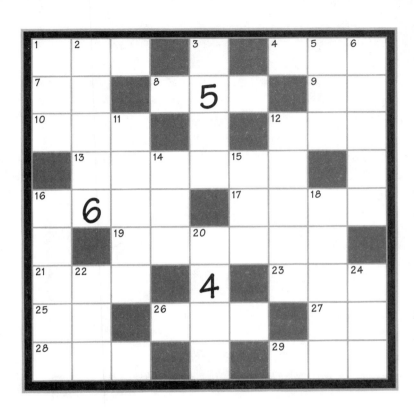

DIRECTIONS

Solve this puzzle as you would a crossword puzzle using numbers instead of words. Only the digits 1 through 9 are used; there are no zeros. Only one digit may be placed in each box, and a digit may be used more than once in an answer. Where it appears that more than one combination of digits is possible, look for additional clues in the interlocking answers. A prime number is divisible only by itself and 1.

CLUES

ACROSS

1. The square of a square (odd)
3. Consecutive digits
5. Consecutive digits out of order
7. Even digits, all different
8. Twelve times a prime number
9. The product of two prime numbers
10. The square of the cube root of 6 down

DOWN

1. A multiple of the square root of 10 Across
2. The sum of the first and third digits is equal to the fourth digit; the second and fifth digits are the same
3. A palindrome of even numbers
4. The cube of a cube (even)
6. A palindrome that is the cube of a prime number
8. A trombone number

Didjaknow... "CHUNKING" HELPS NUMBER RECALL

Most people cannot recall a long series of numbers accurately. The answer is to group two- or three-digit sequences into "chunks."

Answer on page 214

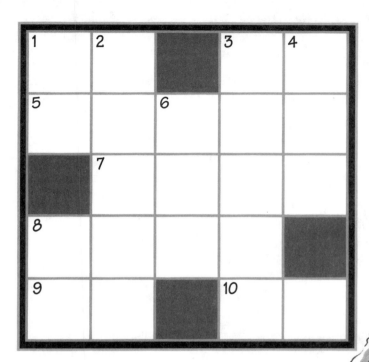

For example, when holding a 10-digit phone number in mind long enough to dial it most people have to group and separate the area code and may combine the remaining single digits into two-digit numbers (6,1,0 as six-ten). They learn social security numbers by memorizing chunks as rhythmic groups, pausing between hyphens.

HINT: 1 Across is 81

Prime Time

DIRECTIONS

Solve this puzzle as you would a crossword puzzle using numbers instead of words. Only the digits 1 through 9 are used; there are no zeros. Only one digit may be placed in each box, and a digit may be used more than once in an answer. Where it appears that more than one combination of digits is possible, look for additional clues in the interlocking answers. A prime number is divisible only by itself and 1.

CLUES

ACROSS

1. The square of the third smallest prime number
3. The square of an Arabic number that looks like a Roman 2
4. An odd number that is 30 less than it would be upside down
6. Onion Market Day in Bern, Switzerland
8. The square of a prime number larger than 1 Across and smaller than 3 Across
9. The next square after 8 Across

DOWN

1. The sum of the last two digits equals the sum of the first three
2. The second and fourth digits are alike
3. The square of an even number that itself is a square
5. The next square after 3 Across
7. The sum of its digits is the square root of 9 Across

Answer on page 214

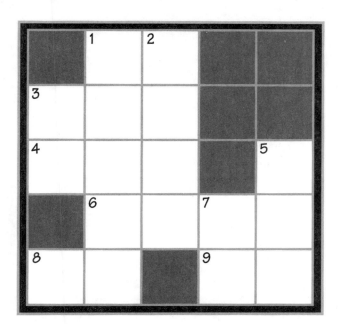

Didjaknow...

SLEEP DEPRIVATION LEADS TO POOR COMPUTATION

A good night's sleep is important for high performance mathematical brain functioning. When math graduates were awakened from recovery sleep after staying up for 48-hours straight, they were unable to calculate even simple math problems. The brain needs adequate sleep in order to compute and answer number equations accurately.

HINT: 6 Across is 1124.

DIRECTIONS

Solve this puzzle as you would a crossword puzzle using numbers instead of words. Only the digits 1 through 9 are used; there are no zeros. Only one digit may be placed in each box, and a digit may be used more than once in an answer. Where it appears that more than one combination of digits is possible, look for additional clues in the interlocking answers. A prime number is divisible only by itself and 1.

CLUES

ACROSS

1. Two more than 8 Down
3. Ten more than 1 Across
5. The first day of winter
7. The seventh day of Chanukah
8. Christmas Day
10. The square of an even number that itself is a cube
11. A multiple of 1 Across

DOWN

2. The square of an odd number
3. The first three digits are alike, so are the last two
4. The sum of the first two digits is equal to the third
6. Boiling point
8. The square of an even number
9. The second digit is double the first

Answer on page 214

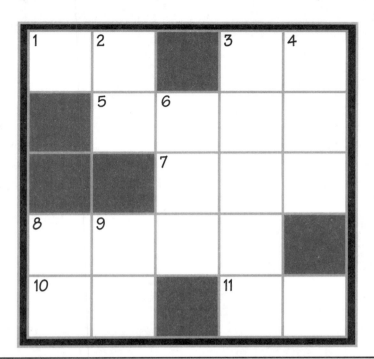

Didjaknow... EINSTEIN'S SPECIAL GENIUS WAS RIGHT-BRAINED

The great physicist was not a genius at math. In school, he struggled with left-brain learning: Computation and language skills (reading, writing and spelling). He did not learn to speak until age three. All his life, most of his thinking was without words. His extraordinary right brain abilities equipped him to visualize concepts into space-time configurations. He labored to translate his insights into mathematics.

HINT: 7 Across is 129

Contributing Factors

DIRECTIONS

Solve this puzzle as you would a crossword puzzle using numbers instead of words. Only the digits 1 through 9 are used; there are no zeros. Only one digit may be placed in each box, and a digit may be used more than once in an answer. Where it appears that more than one combination of digits is possible, look for additional clues in the interlocking answers. A prime number is divisible only by itself and 1.

CLUES

ACROSS

2. Consecutive numbers
4. The cube of an odd number that itself is a square
6. The second digit is the cube of the first
7. A multiple of 8 Down
8. The square of 8 Down
9. The cube of the third smallest possible odd number

DOWN

1. The cube of 8 Down
2. The square of an odd number
3. All even digits: the sum of the first two equals the sum of the last two which are alike
5. See 6 Across
7. A quarter of three
8. The highest common factor of 7 Across

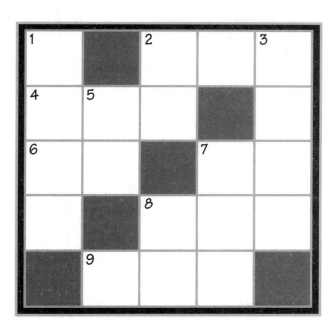

Didjaknow... LEFTIES EXCEL AT COMPUTATION

Studies of left vs. right handers' abilities to solve math tasks attribute lefties' superior performance to their not being right-hemisphere specialized, as most righties are. The areas of the brain that lefties use to process math are more broadly distributed through both hemispheres. Their edge comes from a "more-brain" processing advantage over right-handers for mathematical computation and calculation.

HINT: 4 Across is 729

DIRECTIONS

Solve this puzzle as you would a crossword puzzle using numbers instead of words. Only the digits 1 through 9 are used; there are no zeros. Only one digit may be placed in each box, and a digit may be used more than once in an answer. Where it appears that more than one combination of digits is possible, look for additional clues in the interlocking answers. A prime number is divisible only by itself and 1.

CLUES

ACROSS
1. Consecutive digits
5. A "variety" number
6. The sum of 1 Across and 9 Across
8. The square of a number that itself is a square (even)
9. The reverse of 1 Across

DOWN
2. The square of a number that itself is a square (even)
3. The sum of the first two digits equals the sum of the last three
4. The sum of the first two digits equals the last digit
6. The square of the number that itself is a square (odd)
7. A number divisible by 2 but not by 4

Answer on page 215

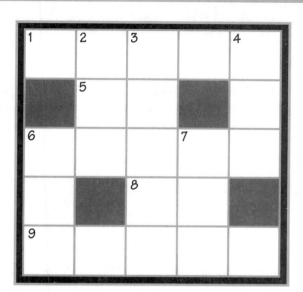

Didjaknow...

HINT: 5 Across is 57.

DIRECTIONS

Solve this puzzle as you would a crossword puzzle using numbers instead of words. Only the digits 1 through 9 are used; there are no zeros. Only one digit may be placed in each box, and a digit may be used more than once in an answer. Where it appears that more than one combination of digits is possible, look for additional clues in the interlocking answers. A prime number is divisible only by itself and 1.

CLUES

ACROSS

1. Consecutive digits, all odd
5. The symmetrical cube of a digit in 1 Across
6. The square of a digit in 1 Across; the sum of its digits equals the root
7. The square of a digit in 1 Across
8. The symmetrical square of a prime number
10. Consecutive digits

DOWN

2. The sum of the first two digits is equal to the sum of the last three
3. Consecutive digits
4. The sum of the last three digits equals the product of the first two
9. The cube of a digit in 1 Across

Answer on page 215

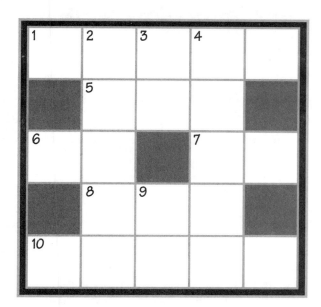

Didjaknow... TESTOSTERONE DECLINE LEADS TO SOME LOSS OF MATH SKILLS

Men tend to be better at math than women, but both will show decline in mathematical ability with age. Brain studies of men show that the hippocampus, a structure that processes math and spatial problems, shrinks more rapidly in men and is directly affected by declining testosterone levels. Since testosterone levels are highest in young adult males, this explains why most math prodigies are males and why these prodigies reach top expertise in their 20's, then decline in ability thereafter.

HINT: Begin with 5 and 8 Across, then 9 Down.

Calculated Surprises

DIRECTIONS

Solve this puzzle as you would a crossword puzzle using numbers instead of words. Only the digits 1 through 9 are used; there are no zeros. Only one digit may be placed in each box, and a digit may be used more than once in an answer. Where it appears that more than one combination of digits is possible, look for additional clues in the interlocking answers. A prime number is divisible only by itself and 1.

CLUES

ACROSS

1. The first year in the second half of the 18th century
4. The symmetrical square of an even number
6. The square of an odd number that itself is a square
7. Half of the largest common factor of 3 Down
8. The sum of the fourth and fifth digits is half the square root of 4 Across; the first three are unities
10. The square of an even number that is one more than the square root of 1 Down

DOWN

1. The square of a prime number whose root is one less than the square root of 10 Across
2. The first two digits are a multiple of the last two
3. Consecutive digits
5. The square of an even number that is four less than the square root of 1 Across
7. The square of 7 Across
9. A prime number

Answer on page 215

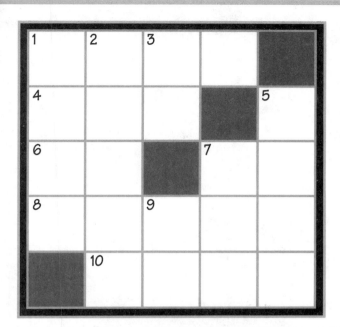

Didjaknow...
NUMBER AND LANGUAGE SKILLS ARE INTERDEPENDENT

Mathematical ability is dependent on language skills in order to name numbers and math formulations. However, language and computation tasks are processed in different areas of the brain. Documented studies have been made of brain-damaged people who can calculate accurately but are not able to name the numbers or operations used in calculation. On the other hand, there are brain-damaged people who can name numbers and count but lack the ability to calculate and answer mathematical problems.

HINT: 1 Across is 1751.

Countdown

Thirteen schoolboys are interested in rugby and want to form a team that will play against other school teams in the city. To choose a captain, they form a circle and will count clockwise by thirteen. Each time thirteen is reached, that boy will drop out of the circle and the count will start again with the boy to his left. Throckmorton Q. Winstead III, who wants to be the captain and is accustomed to getting his own way, volunteers to start the count. Call him A and his friends B through M. With which boy should Throckmorton start counting to assure that he becomes the captain?

Answer on page 215

Didjaknow...

EXPERT CALCULATORS USE BRAIN DIFFERENTLY

Studies done with PET scans compared the brain function of calculating prodigies with a group of regulars. It revealed the relationship between complex mental calculation and memory retrieval of mathematical facts. Results show that prodigies do not show more intense activity in the same areas of the brain non-experts use, but do use *different* brain areas. They can switch between short-term intensive storage strategies and highly proficient memory encoding and retrieval, a process sustained by the right prefrontal and medial temporal brain areas. However, this proficient brain processing weakens with age: most math prodigies hit peak ability in their 20's. (So, if you don't think that the math problem, opposite, is "Entry Level," it may be because you are not still wearing your cap on backwards.)

HINT: *If Throckmorton begins counting with himself he will be the second to leave the circle.*

A greengrocer, whose organic produce market was stocked with good intentions but was losing money, complained to his suppliers that oranges were selling like 1990's tech stocks at 45 cents a pound (a fair price), but no one was buying his grapefruit at 60 cents a pound. Tom suggested that the greengrocer combine the two fruits, bagging them proportionately, and selling them at 50 cents a pound. The greengrocer weighed 20 pounds of grapefruit but had no idea how many oranges would be required. But his supplier, eager to sell his grapefruit, came up with the answer. Can you do this one in your head?

Answer on page 215

Didjaknow...

GAZING TO THE RIGHT STIMULATES MATH SKILLS

Do you dread the approach of April 15th because you have to fill out and file tax forms? Do you put off the monthly act of balancing your checkbook because tasks involving numbers leave you yawning? Next time you have to perform a chore that involves math computation, try placing a plant, picture or cherished item to the right side of your viewing field and glance at it every so often. Researchers say looking to the right stimulates left-brain math skills and should make the process of mathematics flow easier. Go figure — and gaze to the right.

HINT: Use "n" for the required number of pounds. That number times the cost per pound equals the selling price.

Last month when Dick was empanelled for jury duty, Tom volunteered to prepare the invoices based on their hardware store's receipts. He had just one invoice left to do when the electric adding machine suddenly went silent and he was left to his own devices. With a slight shrug of the shoulders, Tom calculated the cost of each item and mailed out the statement shown below. A few days later he received a visit from an irate customer waving his copies of the sales slips. Dick was back from jury duty and saw immediately what Tom had done wrong. All the digits in the cost of each item were either one digit higher or one digit lower than they should have been. For example, Tom wrote down an 8 when he should have written a 7 or 9. In fact, Tom wrote only one of the digits correctly, and that was in the price for the spotlight. Dick corrected the

INVOICE	
Floor Jack	$218.49
Vise	26.81
Spotlight	25.59
	$270.89

Answer on page 215

invoice and the total came to $170 exactly, which saved the customer a little over $100. Can you calculate the correct cost of each of the three items so they total $170?

Didjaknow... SOCIAL FACTORS INFLUENCE MENTAL DISORDERS

Physical and mental health is influenced by our social environment and life experience. A life of "hard times" often causes an early decline in physical health, mental health, and abilities, including computational skills. Those at the low end of the scale, socially and economically, seem to have more problems with certain mental disorders, such as seasonal affective disorder (the "winter blues"), anxiety disorder, and substance abuse. Social and environmental factors such as low birth weight, lack of parental support, abuse and neglect, all influence the development of mental illness and disorders. However, vulnerability also depends on an individual's choices, lifestyle, access to information, and feeling of self-worth.

HINT: Since each digit can be replaced by only another single digit, the nines, if they are only one digit too low, become zeros.

Tom and Dick, hardware dealers extraordinaire, also have a Boy Scout troop. When school was over for the summer they took the troop of thirty-two boys up to the mountains for a few days camping. The shelter was a single large room with space for exactly 14 sleeping bags along each of the four walls. Tom assigned spaces as shown opposite (A). When Dick pointed out that they and the two fathers who were driving

would need space for their sleeping bags as well, he suggested an alternate plan (B).

Then it was remembered that four Boy Scouts had brought along younger brothers who had paid their own way, and the room plan was changed again to accommodate them (C).

All went well until the last night of camping. Four leaders who had been taking a refresher course in wilderness survival asked for shelter from a heavy rainstorm. Again the sleeping bags were moved (D).

At all times the limitation of 14 bags along each wall was met. How did they manage it?

Answer on page 215

A

6	2	6
2	32	2
6	2	6

B

	36	

C

	40	

D

	44	

Didjaknow... BODY AND BRAIN DIFFERENTIATE STRESS

Stressful life events affect the health of the body and the brain. However, there is a difference between generally "feeling stressed out" and real stress. The sympathetic nervous system includes the adrenal glands which produce both adrenaline and cortisol. The autonomic nervous system produces catecholamines and regulates the production of cortisol. Stress such as physical activity, a state of arousal, and fear stimulate adrenaline production. Cortisol production increases in times of more pronounced stress, such as a severe change or threat to one's life, particularly when it is related to an unexpected event and strongly-felt emotions.

HINT: The corner numbers in B are 5

A Bump in the Road

One spring day Willard C. Haskins, a careful and conservative gentleman, fired up his Class C moped to go to the city 15 miles away to get his brush lopper sharpened. This wasn't the fastest transportation available—its top speed was 20 miles per hour—but to a cautious man like Willard, it seemed the most reliable. Willard picked up his sharper lopper and started back at 2 p.m. But after riding two-thirds of the way his rear tire blew so he was forced to walk the remaining distance. Willard arrived home at 3:30 p.m. and his wife demanded to know what had kept him so long. When he explained, in his customary tedious detail, she said he should have walked faster. At what speed did he walk?

Answer on page 215

Didjaknow...

MEMORY IMPROVES WITH VISUALIZING

When an individual memorizes a set of nonfamous faces, against a set of famous faces and pictures of nameable objects, results show memory is very much dependent on a function called coding. The famous faces are remembered better than nonfamous faces, but not noticeably more or less than the nameable objects. For each task, different parts of the brain are used. The nonfamous faces require very strong right hemisphere activation. For the nameable objects and the famous faces, both left and right hemispheres combine efforts to encode information. When both frontal regions are used, memory performance is better than when using only one region.

Therefore, when memorizing a group of unrelated items try to see pictures in your mind, not just hear the words or read the symbols. People with synesthesia, a tendency to attribute sensory data such as musical tones or colors to numbers, words and the names of objects, often have superior memories for this reason

A few years later, Willard and his wife took a trip in their 1991 Chrysler with 163,000 miles on it. She flatly refused to risk her reputation by being seen on the back of his moped with her knees spread. It saddened Willard that she could not share the only flaring spark that had ever entered his life. The only thing that Willard's wife respected about his driving was that he adhered strictly to the posted speed limits that averaged 35 miles per hour on local roads and, at the time, 55 miles per hour on interstate highways. They made their 470-mile trip in ten hours, none too soon for Willard. How much of their driving was on local roads and how much on interstates?

Answer on page 215

Didjaknow...

BOYS AND GIRLS DIFFER IN THE WAY THEY LEARN

In school, the subjects that make girls happy usually make boys miserable. Girls tend to do better and be happier in subjects such as English, writing and foreign languages. The biggest challenge for girls in school tends to be mathematics, with geometry being more difficult than algebra. Boys can do well in math, especially if math is made more spatial. Boys need to apply their physical motor skills to learning, while this does not seem necessary for girls. Some neuroscientists, who are aware of the significant differences in the way female and male brains function and process data, advocate separating the genders for math and language classes, especially in the early and middle grades.

HINT: Their average speed was 12 mph over 35 mph and 8 mph under 55 mph.

CITATIONS

P. 70, 72 Bragdon, A., Gamon, D. (2001) The Brainwaves Center, Bass River, MA.

P. 74 O. Gruber, P. Indefrey, H. Steinmetz, and A. Kleinschmidt.
Cerebral Cortex 2001;11 350-359

P. 76-97 Bragdon, A., Gamon, D. (2001) The Brainwaves Center, Bass River, MA.

P. 99 Lauro Pesenti et al. (2001). Mental calculation in a prodigy is sustained by
right prefrontal and medial temporal areas. Nature Neuroscience 4/1: 103.

P. 101 Kinsbourne, M. (1983). Lateral input may shift activation balance in the
integrated brain. Psychologist 38:228-9.
Levick, S.E. et al. (1993). Asymmetrical visual deprivation: a technique to
differentially influence lateral hemispheric function. Perceptual Motor Skills
76:1363-82.

P. 103 McEwen, Bruce PhD., Head of the Hatch Laboratory of Neuroendocrinology,
Rockefeller University. From a presentation at Science of Cognition
Conference, Library of Congress, Washington, D.C., 6 Oct. 1999.

P. 105 McEwen, Bruce PhD.

P. 107 Petersen, Steven E. PhD.

P. 109 Gur, Ruben C. Sex Differences in Learning. Using Brain Research to Reshape
Classroom Practice. 7-9 Nov.1999.

Section Four

SPATIAL

Visuospatial scratchpad is the term neuroscientists use to refer to a Working Memory tool you will be using when you tackle tasks like the mental exercises on the following pages. Some of the exercises require you to visualize forms in space as architects, builders, sculptors and chess masters must do. In everyday life people use this skill to, for example, fit suitcases into a car's trunk or find their way back to the entrance of a building or relocate their car in the mall parking lot.

The right hemisphere of most male brains is more highly specialized for that kind of skill than the female brain normally is. This is one of the most obvious gender differences in cognitive processing and it seems to correlate with what is known about how protohuman primates lived when their brains were evolving 60 million years ago. Women find their way by identifying landmarks. Men are more likely to orient themselves to large geographical reference points, including the sun and stars. It is tempting to speculate that, as hunters, males traveled long distances drawn by game into unfamiliar territory. Women, who kept close to their dwelling to care for infants and to escape predators, would have been more likely to rely on local landmarks to move around seeking food or firewood in familiar territory near their dwelling.

The visuospatial skills can be developed with practice. A recent neuroscientific study of experienced, professional taxi drivers in London, who are required to pass rigorous tests in finding addresses anywhere in the city before they are licensed, showed that a portion of their brain was significantly larger than that of London workers in other jobs. It is called the *hippocampus*, based on the latin word for horse, (as hippopotamus also is), because at one time somebody must have thought that organ and animal each looked like a horse, (which they don't at all). Every brain has one on each side. The one on the right side, where visuospatial skills are located for most people, was larger in the London cabbies' brains. The neurons in the rear part of that area had sent out more connections to respond to the daily performance demanded of them. This forced an increase in mass which is clearly noticeable in a brain scan.

That finding is a persuasive example of a fact that is little known but is very encouraging. The human brain is able to adapt physically to meet demands put to it, much as a society can change its values in a common crisis or a flower will grow toward the sun's light. This means that the brain responds as other physical systems do. Aerobic exercise builds strength in the heart muscle and oxygen-carrying capacity in the lungs, thereby increasing stamina. Muscle groups gain mass when they are subjected to the regular stresses of targeted exercises. Lifting and running capacity increase as a result. Even if a system has not been used for many years, its mass and effectiveness can be revived with exercise which, incidentally, shows up dramatically in older people who start exercising after leading relatively sedentary lives.

Like life, there is a downside. In the Middle Ages the crafts of architecture, building and draftsmanship — all trades that target the visuospatial centers in the right hemisphere — were known as the melancholy arts because they were thought to depress the spirit. In fact, the right hemisphere does process negative facial expressions and is more active in the depressed phase of a manic-depressive cycle. But that didn't stop Leonardo da Vinci, nor should it you.

DIRECTIONS

A tangram is a Chinese puzzle consisting of a square cut into seven pieces — five triangles, a square, and a rhomboid — which then can be combined to form a great variety of figures. The four tangrams, opposite, have been cut from the square in the upper left-hand corner. They are (we think): a vulture (A); a hand-standing acrobat (B); a man wearing a top hat (C); and a raccoon (D). By drawing lines, can you show how each piece in the original square was used to construct each drawing? Identical pieces have the same numbers and are interchangeable in the drawings

Didjaknow... LESS IS MORE FOR VISUAL STATEMENT

A profile or silhouette often makes a greater visual statement than a color photograph. For example, mystery writer Alfred Hitchcock was easily recognized from an outline of his face; his particulars such as skin and hair texture were insignificant for his recognition since they were similar to any other person's. Because the visual centers in the brain have limited attention resources, oftentimes a simple drawn outline — which communicates less data — is recognized more quickly than a detailed picture.

Answer on page 216

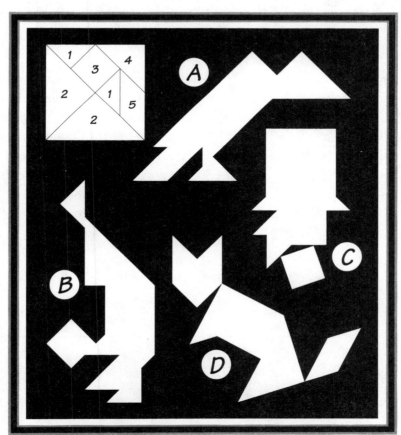

A Piece of Cake

DIRECTIONS

Six hungry boys "borrowed" a white frosted cake from one of their mothers and took it to their secret clubhouse to divide up. But their felonious act had been witnessed by a younger sister and her friend who offered to be silent on the matter in return for a piece of cake each. The boys agreed but set a condition: they would take their pieces first and the girls must select the seventh and eighth pieces in the order the boys had established when they took the first six pieces. The girls quickly saw the pattern and chose the correct seventh piece. Can you?

Didjaknow... SUPERIOR MALE SPATIAL SKILLS MAY BE EVOLUTIONARY

Men are better than women at spatial tasks that involve orientation and navigational skill. This makes sense if you look at evolution, gender role, and survival of our species. During the pre-agricultural hunter-gatherer era, men were primarily hunters and these navigational abilities would be necessary for traveling and tracking game. Women, on the other hand, remained close to home, nursing and tending children.

Answer on page 216

How an individual observes the world visually has more to do with one's ability to notice shapes, shadows and colors than it does with one's personal preferences. Exposure early in life to specific visual experiences — a quilt on a crib, for example — can affect adult taste profoundly, as do social influences such as advertising and peer group choices. The inexperienced eye of a child lacks the invasive social influences that might subconsciously cloud his vision and alter his choices. The part of the right hemisphere that processes abstract, metaphorical associations tends to weaken with age. Individuals with advanced dementia probably would not perceive the social point of the drawing, on the facing page. Can you?

Didjaknow... SEX HORMONES AFFECT THE BRAIN

While male and female brains are different from birth, the hormones of adolescence seem to increase and magnify the differences. Males tend to decline in verbal ability as they go through puberty, whereas females decline in spatial ability. According to Jean Piaget, everyone by the age of 13 should be able to guess the correct answer to his water level test. Interestingly, girls who knew the correct answer to Piaget's water level test at age 11 often lost the answer by age 13 after starting puberty. The only explanation for these changes is that sex hormones produced at adolescence affect both the body and the brain.

Answer on page 216

HINT: Why is the father showing disapproval of the boy's drawing of a curling line?

Checkerboard Square

DIRECTIONS

Think of a 6 x 6 square, or draw one. How many ways can you place 12 checkers, one to a square, so that each row, column, and the two diagonals contain only two checkers?

Didjaknow... MEN ARE BETTER IN SPATIAL ABILITY

Overall results prove that men do better than women on problems involving spatial reasoning and spatial memory. On line orientation tests, where two lines are shown (each set of lines getting shorter), and one must guess if the lines have the same orientation as another set, a man is most likely to guess the correct answer. Piaget's water level test shows a truck traveling uphill one-half filled with water and asks which line represents the level of water. On this test, 45% of men got the answer correct, while only 15% of the women did. When the test grew more difficult, involving a rope remaining perpendicular to the ground, 60% of the men guessed correctly while only 30% of the women did.

Answer on page 216

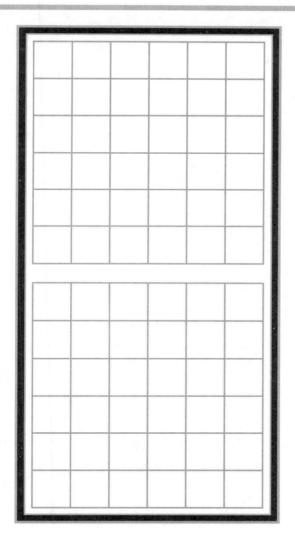

HINT: Of the many possible solutions, one places a checker in each of the corner squares.

Assyrian Miss-tery

DIRECTIONS

Shortly after the artist made this rendering of an ancient Assyrian bas relief, ten pieces mysteriously disappeared. They were recently found in a basement in Bismarck, North Dakota, and put back in their correct positions. The small squares above and below the drawing show the missing pieces. Can you find which sections they belong to? When you locate them, place their letters and numbers in the boxes next to each square. One has already been identified to show how it's done.

Didjaknow... TRANSSEXUALS HAVE BRAIN CHANGE

Sex differences in brain function are due to hormonal influence according to a study done by researchers in the Netherlands. Transsexuals showed the same sex differences in brain function as a biological-born gender. When transsexuals were studied, males that were changed into females declined on spatial ability but improved on verbal functioning. On immediate and delayed memory performance testing, these "new" females tested better than males. Vice versa, females changed to the male gender showed improved spatial ability but declined on verbal fluency. Sex hormones are the only explanation for this phenomenon.

Answer on page 216

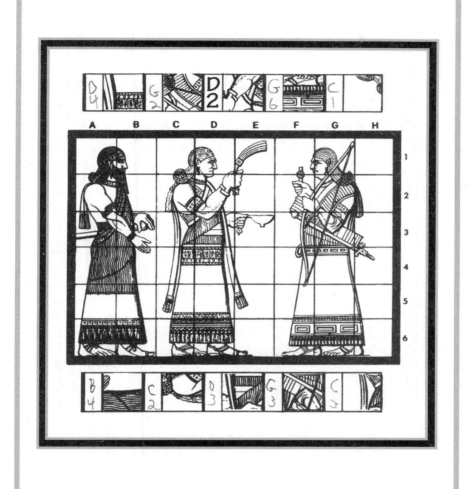

Twice Burned

DIRECTIONS

It can be said that the 40 matches shown, opposite, form 16 squares. It can also be said that they form nine squares made up of four small squares each, four squares of nine squares each, and one large square (the perimeter), making a total of 30 squares altogether.

1. What is the least number of matches that can be removed to eliminate all the squares?

2. Using the matches you removed, can you form six new squares?

Didjaknow... MEN TAKE TO TRAVEL

When couples are traveling, frequently the man is found in the driver's seat. The reason for this customary seating arrangement may have more to do with biology than male chivalry. Brain studies show the circuits specialized for path finding are naturally larger in most male brains than female brains. Males tend to navigate by orientation to general geography and directional clues such as the sun. Females tend to use landmarks along the route more often.

Answer on page 216

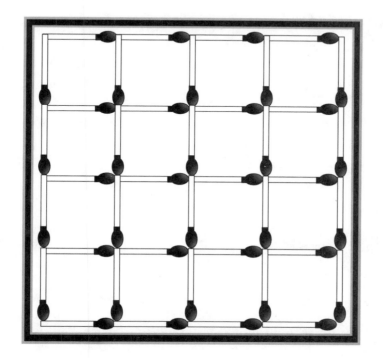

From A to B

DIRECTIONS

All you have to do to solve this puzzle is move in a single, unbroken path from the upper right corner (a) to the lower left corner (b). But, to add a little interest to the problem, your path must take you alternately through square, circle, square, circle, etc. And you may not move diagonally—only vertically and horizontally. We did it in 27 moves. Can you beat that?

Didjaknow... TESTOSTERONE AFFECTS SPATIAL ABILITY

Men are generally better than women at tasks that involve spatial ability. Test results prove that males outperform females on tasks that involve mental rotations of 3-dimensional objects. The reason for this is apparently gender-based and hormonal. Studies were done on infants who were born with the correct male chromosomes (X and Y), yet lacked receptors for the male hormone testosterone. Later in life, school tests showed these males scored lower than "normal" males on tests involving spatial and mathematical skills.

Answer on page 216

Unexpected Windfall

T he brothers Tom and Dick were invited to Cousin Harry's wedding which was being held in Hurley, 300 miles away. They decided to drive nonstop, alternating the driving. A heavy rainstorm with high winds followed them for several hours. Shortly before sundown, "in the middle of nowhere," they passed through the town of Burley and suddenly came to an intersection where the signpost had been knocked down by the wind. Tom, who was at the wheel, didn't know which way the sign had been pointing, although the town of Hurley was shown on it. He began berating his brother for not bringing

a road map. Dick got out of the car for a few minutes, then got back in and told Tom which road to take. How did he know which way was the correct one?

Answer on page 216

Didjaknow...

EXPLORING NEW AVENUES MAKES THE BRAIN GROW

Here's a new excuse to plan an excursion out of town: exploring new avenues will challenge the brain and literally help it grow. A brain-scan study of London cabbies shows the rear of the hippocampus, a seat of spatial memory, is larger than in other drivers, relative to years of experience. The same area of the hippocampus grows larger in birds forced to learn new navigational or food finding skills. If you've been thinking of finding your way out of town or cross-country, go for it! Traveling that involves mapping out and navigating works your spatial memory.

Crunchy Cake

DIRECTIONS

When you celebrate a birthday in the land of Klunk, it is customary to embed coins of various denominations rather than candles in the icing of the birthday cake. Moreover, the guest of honor must cut the cake in such a way that the coins amount to the same total in every piece. Of course, this usually results in some very peculiar-looking pieces of cake. If it were your birthday and you had six guests, how would you cut the cake so the coins in all seven pieces would equal the same total?

Didjaknow... BRAIN ENJOYS VISUAL BINDING AND DISCOVERY TASKS

For survival, vision evolved so an individual is able to discern camouflaged objects. In order to do this, the brain has to assemble partially-hidden pieces of visual data into a recognizable object. For example, if we view a coyote behind green shrubbery, our visual brain links all the gray areas, combining them together to create the coyote's image. The very nature of this task seems to be a pleasing one: scientists indicate this binding and discovery process creates a positive emotional response, possibly by sending signals directly to our limbic brain where emotions originate.

Answer on page 216

DIRECTIONS

Tom has always been interested in the electric tools he and his brother Dick carry in their hardware store. On one slow day recently he took out a piece of graph paper and began planning a layout for a parquet counter-top insert. It would be composed of eight L-shaped pieces of veneer fitted together to form a square, but after several attempts he was ready to give up. Dick watched for a while, then suggested cutting four L shapes and four Z shapes. Do you know how these can be arranged to form a square.

Didjaknow...   CARICATURES SUBTRACT AND AMPLIFY

When a rat is rewarded for responding to a rectangle instead of a square, the rat's response to a longer and narrower rectangle is even greater, due to a cognitive principle called the "peak-shift" effect. Artists rely on the same cognitive rule when they produce caricature art. When a cartoonist draws a caricature of a famous face, such as Yasser Arafat, the artist visualizes the average of all faces and subtracts that from Arafat's face. By rendering the differences, the finished drawing exaggerates features, creating a sketch that looks more like Arafat than Arafat himself.

Answer on page 217

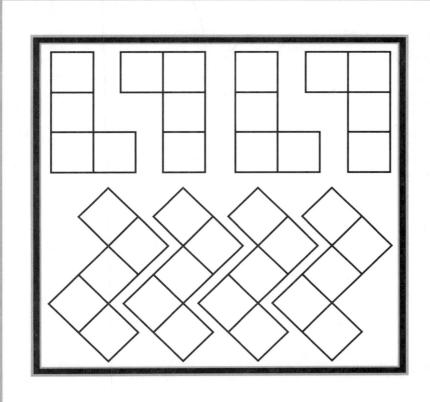

CITATIONS

P. 114 Ramachandran, V.S. MD, PhD. Professor and Director, Center for Brain and Cognition, University of California-San Diego. From a presentation at the Science of Cognition Conference. Library of Congress. Washington, D. C., 6 Oct. 1999.

P. 116 Bragdon, Allen D. The Brainwaves Center, Bass River, MA (2001).

P. 118 Gur, Ruben C. Sex Differences in Learning. Using Brain Research to Reshape Classroom Practice. Public Information Resources, Inc. 7-9 Nov. 1999.

P. 120, 122 Gur, Ruben C.

P. 124 Maguire, E.A. et al. (2000). Navigation-related structural changes in the hippocampi of taxi drivers. Proceedings of the National Academy of Sciences USA 97/8:4398-403.
Clayton, N.S., and J.R. Krebs (1994). Hippocampal growth and attrition in birds affected by experience. Proceedings of the National Academy of Sciences USA 91:7410-14.

P. 126 Bragdon, Allen and Gamon, David PhD. "Building Left Brain Power," Brainwaves Books, Bass River, MA (2000).

P. 129 Maguire, E.A. et al. (2000).

P. 130, 132 Ramachandran, V.S. MD, PhD.

Section Five
LANGUAGE

Have you heard about the latest brain research? If you stimulate your brain with cognitive challenges, you'll raise its dopamine levels. Dopamine is a neurotransmitter produced by the brain to facilitate passing signals among brain cells. Dopamine also makes you feel good by causing a rewarding sense of satisfaction, especially when the brain works on a left-hemisphere task like a word task. The same stimulus-reward system is activated by some narcotics. (Does that make us "pushers"?) Your brain loves to feel good. If it can't do it by solving puzzles, it'll look for other means. The puzzles are generally better for you than the other means that don't add to your vocabulary much.

Consider, just for a moment, how lucky we humans are to be able to learn our language all by ourselves at such an early age that we think life is *supposed* to be that much work. Infants and young children learn the basic structure, pronunciation, grammar and most of the vocabulary of their native language independently of the teaching skills of their parents. Self-education in acquisition of a skill that complex is a stroke of brilliance in brain design. Recruiting a self-motivating neurotransmitter like dopamine as a player in that process is a second masterstroke. Together, they seem to verify that brain design, like the design of a lasting political Constitution, requires a realistic appraisal of human motivations and self-interest.

English is trickier than most languages. It is harder to read, write, and spell English words, and make sense of fast-moving conversation and printed paragraphs. The incidence of dyslexia, for example, is lower in non-English-speaking communities. The difference is not schooling, it is the consistency of the language. The

40-odd sounds in English can be written in over 1000 different ways. The brain has to work faster to decode English sentences ("Does that "gh" sound like an "ff" in tough or "gas" in ghastly, or what?). In Italian, for example, you get just what you see, every time. The fact that Italy has half as many dyslexic children per capita as the U.S. may be because the human brain can decode the sounds of an Italian sentence milliseconds faster than the same sentence in English. Milliseconds count in processing word comprehension of a new language — a child in preschool could tell you that (as soon as he learns to speak his native tongue, of course).

What part of your brain will you be exercising in this Section of the book? Left, mostly. The right side is more active in Sections 4 and 6. Word processing may seem exclusively left-brain linear because you must keep track of sound- and meaning-units produced in rapid sequence. Some aspects of language recall are linear, but not all. You can't "get" verbal jokes or puns unless you hold multiple ideas in your head at once — an ability shared by the front part of both hemispheres, but mostly the right. Incidentally, the burst of laughter that follows a good joke also enlists circuits of stimulus and reward. The stimulus is to search for how the surprising punch line *does* follow the set-up story line. When the punch-line hits, your brain relishes scurrying around to figure out how the unexpected fits. The reward part comes when you "get" it.

We designed these exercises to help you feel good and stay smart. Few other things in life that are so good for you are this much fun.

Fowl Advice

DIRECTIONS

To find the words to a wise old adage, start with the top word in each column and change one letter as you go down the ladder. The dot in the box shows which letter needs to be changed. Letters do not change position with any move. The Mystery Words at the bottom of the ladders, when solved and arranged in the correct sequence, will form a well-known saying.

Didjaknow... STROKES IN THE LEFT BRAIN OFTEN DAMAGE LANGUAGE CENTERS

In America over half a million people suffer brain damage from strokes each year and one-quarter of those are fatal. Disturbances in speech and language comprehension are often observed when a stroke occurs in the left hemisphere of the brain. A stroke happens when the brain's blood supply is blocked due to a break or clot in a blood vessel. Brain cells that are deprived of oxygen die within minutes, releasing certain chemicals that trigger a chain reaction that is harmful to surrounding brain tissue. Language-processing cells that are only stunned, not killed, often regain their function in time. In younger people, especially, other parts of the brain will take over language speaking or comprehension tasks from damaged areas where those functions are normally processed.

Answer on page 217

BAGS

B	A	G	S
R	A	G	S
R	A	T	S
R	U	T	S
G	u	t	s
G	i	t	s
w	i	t	s
w	i	t	h

(1)

FIX

F	I	X
F	i	n
D	i	n
D	u	n
D	u	d
B	u	d
B	u	n
B	a	n

(2)

SHINE

S	H	I	N	E
s	p	I	N	E
s	p	i	r	e
s	p	a	r	e
s	h	a	r	e
s	h	o	r	e
s	h	o	n	e

(3)

ANY

A	N	Y
A	N	t
A	N	D
A	D	D
A	D	E
O	D	E
O	N	E

(4)

SAVE

S	A	V	E

(5)

CORNY

C	O	R	N	Y

(6)

HINT: The answer to Mystery Word 4 is ONE.

Thoughtful Browsing

DIRECTIONS

To find the words to an old adage, start with the top word in each column and change one letter as you go down the ladder. The dot in the box shows which letter needs to be changed. Letters do not change position with any move. The Mystery Words at the bottom of the ladders, when solved and unscrambled, will form a well-known saying. Cognitive Chick is holding an extra Mystery Word that is used in the saying, and she has started one ladder to get you going.

Didjaknow... LEARNING DISABILITIES CAN OFTEN BE OUTGROWN

Parents and teachers often see children who do not fit common definitions of learning disabilities. Like faces, our brains differ in arrangement and proportion. Some children with learning disabilities actually have brain anomalies which, in certain cases, can actually be outgrown. When a child shows symptoms of abnormal behavior, such as poor language skill, it could be due to brain areas that are not fully developed or are developing abnormally. In a young person, new circuits may be able to replace the abnormal ones and language skills will eventually be mastered. However, if all the language centers have fully matured and the disability has not been overcome, the deficit is likely to be permanent.

Answer on page 217

T	O
L	O
L	A
H	A
H	I
2	

R	U	L	E
3			

R	O	D	E
4			

R	I	D
5		

A	R	T
6		

R	O	P	E	S
7				

H	O	L	E
8			

HINT: The answer to Mystery Word 5 is YOU.

Good Horse Sense

DIRECTIONS

To find the words to an old adage, start with the top word in each column and change one letter as you go down the ladder. The dot in the box shows which letter needs to be changed. Letters do not change position with any move. The Mystery Words at the bottom of the ladders, when solved and unscrambled, will form a well-known saying. Cognitive Chick is holding two extra Mystery Words that are used in the saying, and she has started one ladder to get you going.

Didjaknow... COMPLEX SENTENCES CAN CONFUSE

Read the following: "The dog that mother just fed bit the cat." "Mother just fed the dog that bit the cat." Most likely, you found the first sentence harder to understand. PET scans reveal that complex sentences create a greater load on the frontal lobes where Working Memory is. Although a complicated writing style may ward off dementia because it works the brain, it is best not to confuse readers. When writing or speaking, avoid using sentences that require keeping one idea in mind while reading or hearing another idea in the same sentence.

Answer on page 217

T	O	E
T	O	O
W	O	O
W	H	O
W	h	y
T	h	y
3 T	h	e

R	A	C	E
L	a	c	e
L	a	c	k
L	o	c	k
B	o	c	k
B	o	o	k
4 L	o	o	k

R	O	B	E	D
R	o	w	e	d
S	o	w	e	d
S	e	w	e	d
S	e	w	e	r
S	e	v	e	r
5 N	e	v	e	r

T	I	R	E
T	i	m	e
L	i	m	e
L	i	f	e
r	i	f	e
R	i	f	t
6 G	i	f	t

L	O	O	K	S
B	O	O	K	s
B	o	o	t	s
B	o	o	t	h
S	o	o	t	h
S	O	u	t	h
7 m	o	u	t	h

P	O	I	S	E
N	O	i	s	e
N	O	O	s	e
M	O	O	s	e
M	O	u	s	e
H	O	u	s	e
8 h	O	r	s	e

HINT: The answer to Mystery Word 5 is NEVER.

Doggoned Right!

DIRECTIONS

To find the words to an old adage, start with the top word in each column and change one letter as you go down the ladder. The dot in the box shows which letter needs to be changed. Letters do not change position with any move. The Mystery Words at the bottom of the ladder, when solved and unscrambled, will form a well-known saying. Cognitive Chick is holding an extra Mystery Word that is used in the saying, and she has started one ladder to get you going.

Didjaknow...

GOOD READING SKILLS ARE ACUTELY ACQUIRED AND REQUIRED

Because today's electronic society is so dependent on printed information, the development and acquisition of good reading skills, learned during the early years, is more important than ever. However, reading, unlike speaking, relies on abilities that must be meticulously taught. To acquire the skill for reading, children must become aware of the relationship between print and sound, and children have to recognize how sounds combine to create words. For example, children must understand that "dog" while spoken and heard as one continuous sound, is actually composed of three letter-sounds that can be rearranged to produce still other words with different sounds and meanings. Dyslexia is the result of impairment in that very phonological ability.

Answer on page 217

ANT	SET	BURN	BUT
A N D	B E T	B o r n	B I T
A D D	B A T	B o r e	B I N
A D E	M A T	B a r e	T I N
O D E	M E T	C a r e	t o n
O D D	N E T	C a r t	y o n
2 O L D	3 N E W	4 c a m t	5 y o u

SUN	CRAVED	HITCH
S O N	B r a v e d	H a t c h
T O N E	B r a c e d	H u n c h
T O E	T r a c e d	B u n c h
t o e	T r a c e s	b e n c h
D O E	t r a c k s	b e a c h
6 D o g	7 T r i c k s	8 t e a c h

Colorful Conundrum

DIRECTIONS

Start at a single letter (A, I, or E) and add two letters to it to spell a three-letter word in the next row. Continue until you complete the colorful (or colorless) Mystery Word at the end of the ladder. You may rearrange the letters to spell each new word. Work the center puzzle from the single letter I to the top, and the other two, from A and E, to the bottom. No proper nouns, abbreviated, hyphenated, or foreign words are allowed. Each letter falling in a circle is worth the number of points shown in the "Letter Values" column on the opposite page. Try to complete words that offer the highest score.

Didjaknow... DYSLEXIA MAY BE A PHONOLOGICAL PROBLEM

By asking a child to translate words into Pig Latin, scientists can measure the ability to identify sounds in words. This phonological test requires recognizing the first sound of a word, moving it to the end of the word, and adding an additional sound. To achieve this task, a child must be able to remember the word substructure ready for manipulation, just as he must remember sounds while sounding out a new word. When attempting this task, dyslexic children take significantly longer and make more errors than children with good reading skills. While attempting to read, some dyslexic children not only report visual complaints, such as "the words seem to be moving," but many also experience and report difficulties linking a written syllable with its sound.

ISLEXIADAY

Answer on page 217

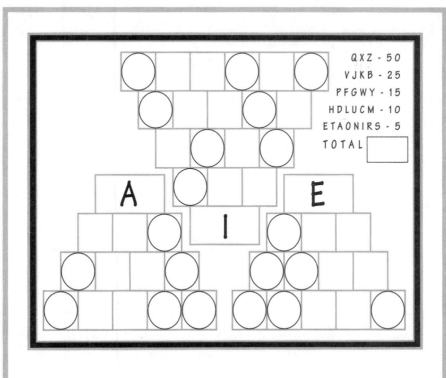

QXZ - 50
VJKB - 25
PFGWY - 15
HDLUCM - 10
ETAONIRS - 5
TOTAL

A   E   I

DIRECTIONS

Start at a single letter (E, A, or I) and add a letter to it to spell a two-letter word in the next row. Then add a letter to spell a three-letter word in the third row. Continue until you complete the six-letter word in the sixth row. You may rearrange the letters to spell each new word. Work the center puzzle from the single letter A to the top, and the other two, from E and I, to the bottom. No proper nouns, abbreviated, hyphenated, or foreign words are allowed. Each letter falling in a circle has the number of points shown in the "Letter Values" column. When all three diagrams are completed, use any six letters from the three six-letter words and spell out a new six-letter word in the Winner-Word box. Each of these letters is worth DOUBLE their letter value. Then add up your circled-letter points and your Winner-Word points and write your answer in the Total box.

Didjaknow... LEFT BRAIN LIKES FAMILIAR SYMBOLS

While the left hemisphere tends to be verbal and the right hemisphere tends to be visual, these abilities are not completely specialized to one side. Familiar icons and symbols, such as letters of the alphabet or a handicap symbol, are automatically processed by the left-brain. Less familiar visual images, such as a strange face or odd-shaped object, are handled more on the right side of the brain. Even a foreign language that uses unfamiliar symbols, such as the Chinese alphabet, would first be processed by the right brain.

Answer on page 218

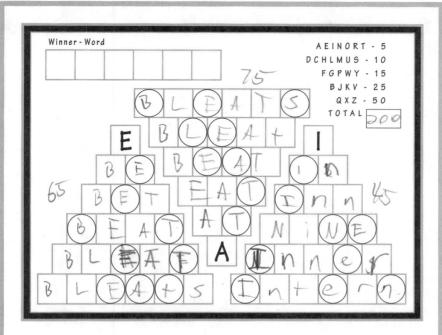

Winner-Word

AEINORT - 5
DCHLMUS - 10
FGPWY - 15
BJKV - 25
QXZ - 50
TOTAL

How close can you come to our total?

Within 100 points — Excellent

Within 150 points — Good

Within 200 points — Fair

Within 300 points — Better use a dictionary!

HINT: Our six-letter word at the bottom of the E ladder is DAZZLE.

DIRECTIONS

Rearrange each group of letters to form a different word, then place the new words in the grid, starting each in its numbered square, so that each word reads the same across and down, e.g., 1 Across and 1 Down read the same, 2 Across and 2 Down read the same, etc. Clues to the correct words for all five groups are given in parentheses.

Didjaknow... LEARNING DISABILITIES ARE DETERMINED BY SOCIETY

A learning disability is defined as a cognitive function that is disproportionately weak and causes a problem in some activity of daily living. Many people compensate for a functional weakness by using other abilities and, therefore, are never evaluated or diagnosed as having a learning disability. A learning disability is actually defined by the society you are living in. American society does not test for musical ability, for example, because it does not require a citizen to become an accomplished musician. However, reading is considered necessary to function in our society, so those who lack the ability to read need to be evaluated for a possible learning disability.

Answer on page 218

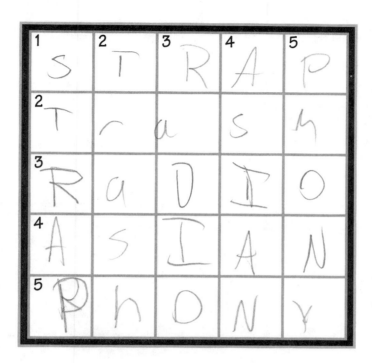

1 S	2 T	3 R	4 A	5 P
2 T	r	a	s	h
3 R	a	D	I	O
4 A	S	I	A	N
5 P	h	O	N	Y

CLUES

1. PARTS (looped band)
2. RHATS (rubbish)
3. DORIA (British wireless)
4. INASA (Thai, e.g.)
5. YONHP (fake)

DIRECTIONS

Rearrange each group of letters to form a different word, then place the new words in the grid, starting each in its numbered square, so that each word reads the same across and down, e.g., 1 Across and 1 Down read the same, 2 Across and 2 Down read the same, etc. Clues to the correct words for three of the groups are given in parentheses.

Didjaknow... WRITING TEST REVEALS LEFT-HANDED THINKING

Although most left-handers process language in the right hemisphere of their brains, this is not true for all lefties. If you are left handed, a team of scientists say a simple writing test can reveal which side of the brain controls your language skills: If you write with your left hand *below* the line of writing, as right-handers do, your dominant language hemisphere is opposite from your writing hand (therefore right); if you write with your hand in a hooked position *above* the line, then your left brain is processing language as it normally does for right-handed people.

Answer on page 218

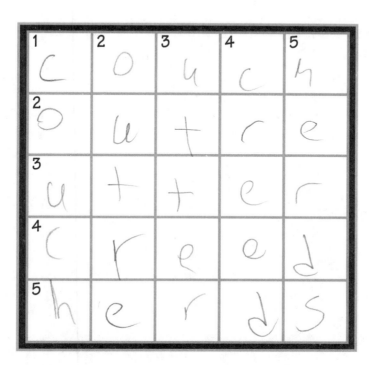

1	2	3	4	5
C	o	u	c	h
o	u	t	r	e
u	t	t	e	r
c	r	e	e	d
h	e	r	d	s

CLUES

1. CHUCO (sofa)
2. ROUTE (extreme, Fr.)
3. TRUET
4. ECERD
5. DERSH (groups)

DIRECTIONS

Rearrange each group of letters to form a different word, then place the new words in the grid, starting each in its numbered square, so that each word reads the same across and down, e.g., 1 Across and 1 Down read the same, 2 Across and 2 Down read the same, etc. Clue to one correct word in the five groups is given in parentheses.

Didjaknow... "LIKE WHATEVER" HINDERS TEENS

All teenagers develop peer lingo, but if jargon slows vocabulary growth, it may limit the future. The average 14-year-old knows about 20,000 words. If learning continues at this rate, by age 64, the vocabulary will consist of 100,000 words (half of Webster's dictionary). To achieve this, a teen has to learn approximately 150 new words a month. Asking your adolescent to use alternate words for "like, whatever" forces the developing brain to organize and use information more precisely. Benefits are numerous. Besides building brain power, the increased vocabulary boosts fluidity of verbal expression and reading skills, thus leading to better job prospects. Studies also show that an increased vocabulary may reduce the risk for Alzheimer's.

Answer on page 218

1 C	2 R	3 E	4 T	5 E
2 R	a	v	e	n
3 E	V	E	N	T
4 T	e	n	s	e
5 E	N	T	e	R

CLUES

1. ERECT
2. NVEAR (bird)
3. NTEEV

4. NTEES
5. NTEER

Agree to Be Anxious

DIRECTIONS

Rearrange each group of letters to form a different word, then place the new words in the grid, starting each in its numbered square, so that each word reads the same across and down, e.g., 1 Across and 1 Down read the same, 2 Across and 2 Down read the same, etc.

Didjaknow...

MUCH LIKE CHOCOLATE AND DRUGS ...

...jokes stimulate the reward-processing centers within the brain. Researchers know that a "good" joke involves two elements: 1. juxtaposing two mental sets (first, setting up a simple situation, then supplying an unexpected twist, often called the "punch line") and, 2. creating in a listener a feeling of being amused. With today's technology, these events can actually be observed as they happen in the brain. While undergoing fMRI brain scan imaging, subjects listened to "punch-line" jokes and puns, signaling when they found the items amusing. At the "feeling of humor" stage, images revealed activity in the medial ventral prefrontal cortex, a region of the brain known as the reward processing center which also shows activity in the stimulus-reward cycles of alcohol, drugs and some sweets.

Answer on page 218

	1	2	3	4	5
1	C	h	e	s	t
2	h	e	a	t	h
3	l	a	g	e	r.
4	S	T	e	e	R
5	T	h	r	e	e

CLUES

1. TSECH
2. THEHA
3. AGREE

4. EETSR
5. ETHER

HINT: The answer to 4 is STERE.

DIRECTIONS

In this crossword puzzle format, you will use each letter of the alphabet only once.

Didjaknow... APOE-4 MAY FORETELL ALZHEIMER'S

The risk for Alzheimer's may be revealed on fMRI scans. Subjects with the APOE-4 (*apolipoloprotein* E-4) gene variant linked to Alzheimer's disease were given memory performance tests while being scanned. Results were compared to subjects without the gene, with all subjects scoring normally on standard memory tests. When asked to recall a pair of learned words, scans showed increased blood flow to several brain regions: the language areas, prefrontal cortex, and temporal lobe-limbic connection which includes the hippocampus. The APOE-4 subjects showed greater blood flow and activity over larger, diversified brain areas, yet no relative increase in performance was seen. Two years later, memory testing and scans of the same subjects showed that the more circuits the brain engaged, the greater the decline in verbal memory. Scientists believe the increased brain activity observed in these patients can predict further brain depreciation to come.

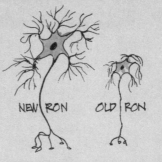

Answer on page 218

CLUES

ACROSS

2. Football venue
5. Harm
7. TV spot, e.g.
9. Surname prefix
10. Sleeveless garment

DOWN

1. Difficult situation
3. The yoke's on him
4. Medical malefactor
6. St.
8. Turkish topper

HINT: 1 Down is PLIGHT.

Bard's Hasty Dame

DIRECTIONS

In this crossword puzzle format, you will use each letter of the alphabet only once.

Didjaknow... MISSPELLING MAY BE A WORKING MEMORY PROBLEM

Studies were conducted on people who tend to misspell the final part of words. The probability of making an error increased with the length of the word and did not depend on whether the subject was asked to type, write, or verbally spell the word. This deficit occurred even when subjects could verbally repeat the word and could correctly spell short words. Results of tests revealed that misspelling the final part of words is actually a *Working Memory* deficit. Working Memory uses two tools to hold information in mind while working additional parts of a problem: the *phonological loop* (hearing words for data with mind's ear); and the *visuospatial scratch-pad* (seeing info with mind's eye). If a person cannot "see, hear, and hold" the first part of a word active in memory for further processing, the end of the word will often be misspelled.

Answer on page 218

CLUES

ACROSS

3. Spar
4. Water lily leaf
6. Apace
7. Automobile corp.
9. Gusto

DOWN

1. Accompanied (with)
2. Lower jaw
4. Parti Québécois (abbr.)
5. Faint
8. Western st.

HINT: 2 Down is JOWL.

Reversed Bet

DIRECTIONS

In this crossword puzzle format, you will use each letter of the alphabet only once.

Didjaknow... "SOUNDS" OF WORDS NOT NECESSARY FOR WRITING?

Must you hear the sounds of a word in your mind in order to write and spell? Neuroscientists are still fighting over that issue. There are two theories regarding the relationship of "sounding" and writing words. One theory, referred to as the "phonological mediation" hypothesis, claims a person *must* mentally hear the sounds of a word in order to correctly write it. On the other hand, the "orthographic autonomy" hypothesis states one does *not* need to mentally sound a word in order to write it. Evidence supporting this second theory was observed in a 60-year old with progressive frontotemporal dementia — this patient could not sound out words, yet was able to correctly write them.

Answer on page 218

CLUES

ACROSS

3. Supported
4. Paper meas.
5. Mot
6. Good-natured banter
8. ___ Affair, 1797-1798

DOWN

1. Seductive flirt
2. Not many
3. With radiance
7. Switch position

HINT: 3 Across is BACKED.

Ditch That Truck!

DIRECTIONS

In this crossword puzzle format, you will use each letter of the alphabet only once. To make things a little more interesting, we've omitted the black squares.

CLUES

ACROSS

3. Kipling poem
4. Disreputable joint
6. Popular gait
8. An R of R&R
10. Wildcat
11. Electrical abbr.

DOWN

1. ___ code
2. "_____ the Raven…"
4. Music emcees
5. British sports car
7. _____ Hills, SD
8. MD's asst.
9. Former
12. Foreign car mfr.

Didjaknow... LEFT BRAIN USUALLY LEARNS LANGUAGE

Researchers think that language is generally processed in the left hemisphere of the brain because during infancy the right hemisphere is busy processing early, less complicated information. As an infant matures and cognition increases, the left hemisphere is accessible and ready to take on the detailed and specialized processing that language learning involves.

Answer on page 218

Starboard Tack

DIRECTIONS

Arguments begin when one word leads to another, and in this puzzle words not only lead to each other, but often overlap. If you start in slot #1 with the right word and continue clockwise you should have little trouble completing the circle with 18 additional words. Each word starts in a numbered slot that corresponds to the number of the clue.

CLUES

1. Show biz headliner
2. Sour
3. Ostentatiously artistic
4. Hollywood Power
5. Bragging rights number
6. Impudent effrontery
7. Old soldier
8. Engrave
9. Moonstruck actress?
10. Not his
11. Formerly (Arch.)
12. Thrust; plunge
13. Competent
14. Horse : whinny : : sheep : ___
15. Suede
16. Not here
17. Schismatic belief
18. In ___ (agreeing)
19. Treasure repository

Didjaknow... WATCHING WHERE THE WORDS ARE

Before the development of MRI scanning technology in 1985, neuro-scientists could not watch as the brain processes language tasks in real time. They knew, for example, that damage to the left frontal lobe

Answer on page 219

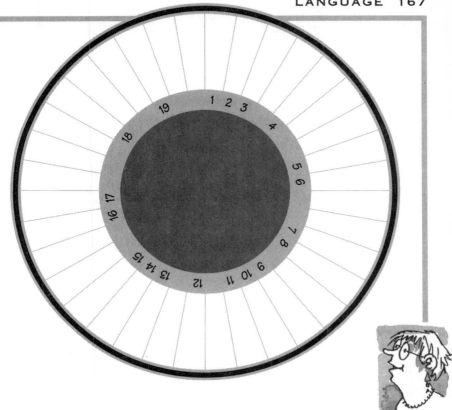

generally correlated with an inability to speak. Now they can see what all parts of a live brain are doing *while they are doing it*. For example, it is possible to observe how the right side of a child's brain attempts to take over a language function of the left side which has been damaged by accident or inheritance.

HINT: 12 is STAB.

Bah Humbug!

DIRECTIONS

Arguments begin when one word leads to another, and in this puzzle words not only lead to each other, but often overlap. If you start in slot #1 with the right word and continue clockwise you should have little trouble completing the circle with 14 additional words. Each word starts in a numbered slot that corresponds to the number of the clue.

Didjaknow... FEMALE BRAIN MORE LIKELY TO USE BOTH SIDES FOR LANGUAGE

Until recently, scientists thought that most people process language in the left hemisphere of the brain. Now researchers know this generalization is more valid for men than for women. Apparently, women's verbal processing areas are more likely to be distributed throughout both sides of the brain. Female patients with injury or strokes to the left hemisphere of the brain show fewer language deficits than males and are better able to recover language skills.

Answer on page 219

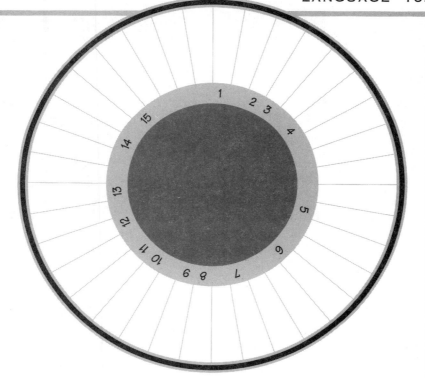

CLUES

1. Audio distortion
2. ___ of the cloth (ecclesiastic)
3. S.A. mountain range
4. Fate
5. Lesser goddess
6. Irrational fear
7. Prejudice
8. Inquire
9. Pervert; distort
10. Ram's mate
11. Existed once
12. Take up again
13. Staircase post
14. Mischievous
15. Complete

HINT: 6 is PHOBIA

Bespoke in Spokane

DIRECTIONS

Arguments begin when one word leads to another, and in this puzzle words not only lead to each other, but often overlap. If you start in slot #1 with the right word and continue clockwise you should have little trouble completing the circle with 17 additional words. Each word starts in a numbered slot that corresponds to the number of the clue.

CLUES

1. Wheel part
2. Understanding
3. Stage direction
4. Dist.
5. Off course
6. Rave's partner
7. Part of the pot
8. Try
9. High regard
10. Aswarm
11. Blend; participate
12. Faint light
13. Saunter
14. Rent
15. Delineate sharply
16. Dear in Nantes
17. Thyme, e.g.
18. Engaged to be married

Didjaknow... TWO CODES ARE BETTER THAN ONE

Memory can be divided into three temporal stages. In the first , the encoding stage, information (visual and/or verbal) is presented. During the second stage, information is stored and frequently reinforced. The third, or retrieval, stage occurs when stored information is remembered.

Answer on page 219

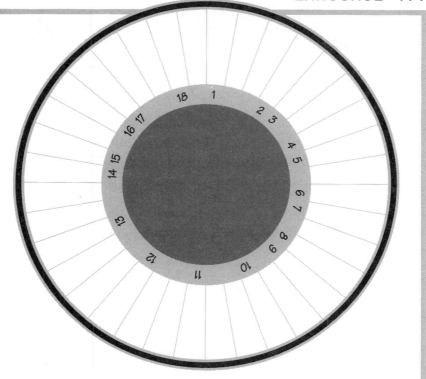

You are more likely to remember an object if you are shown a picture of it, rather than just hearing the word that names the object. For example, when you see a picture of an object such as a lizard, you are encoding visual information plus the name "lizard." If you are asked to remember the object later, the visual and verbal codes combine to give you a better memory than one single code of just a simple word.

HINT: 11 is MINGLE.

DIRECTIONS

Arguments begin when one word leads to another, and in this puzzle words not only lead to each other, but often overlap. If you start in slot #1 with the right word and continue clockwise you should have little trouble completing the circle with 16 additional words. Each word starts in a numbered slot that corresponds to the number of the clue.

Didjaknow... FALSE WORDS IMPAIR FACTS

Language is a valuable tool for communication, thought, and memory. However, when describing an object or event, such as an accident or a car, if the words create incorrect descriptive values and images, they can actually impair later recognition of the actual car and create false beliefs of the factual event. This happens because an inaccurate verbal description can often override a more precise nonverbal memory.

Answer on page 219

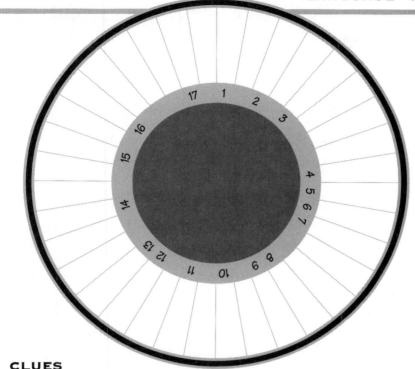

CLUES

1. ___ egg (retirement fund perhaps)
2. Baby bird
3. Scottish islands
4. Ogle
5. Affirmative
6. City in NE Italy
7. Vapor
8. Etiquette's Vanderbilt
9. Talking bird
10. Kind of tag
11. Nourishing occasion
12. Mohammed ___
13. Schulz character
14. More than often
15. Bedfellow
16. Kind of poem
17. Flog

HINT: 9 is MYNA.

Chock–Full o' Mots

DIRECTIONS

Arguments begin when one word leads to another, and in this puzzle words not only lead to each other, but often overlap. If you start in slot #1 with the right word and continue clockwise you should have little trouble completing the circle with 21 additional words. Each word starts in a numbered slot that corresponds to the number of the clue.

Didjaknow... VACCINE MAY HOLD HOPE FOR ALZHEIMER'S

Alzheimer's disease often causes loss of language skills frequently leading to speechlessness. New studies show that a protein-like chemical called *amyloid beta peptide* plays a critical role in the events leading to Alzheimer's. During the first stage of the disease, deposits of amyloid beta peptide build up plaque in spaces between brain cells. In response, the nerve cells develop fibrous tangles and eventually die, causing the brain to shrink. Recent research reveals that mice with Alzheimer's recovered their ability to learn a task and remember it after being vaccinated with amyloid beta peptide. These vaccinated mice appear to create antibodies that help to destroy some of the plaque buildup in the brain. However, because amyloid beta peptide is part of a protein that occurs naturally in humans, researchers do not yet know if the antibodies will cause a harmful reaction to healthy tissues, thus making the vaccine unfit for humans.

Answer on page 219

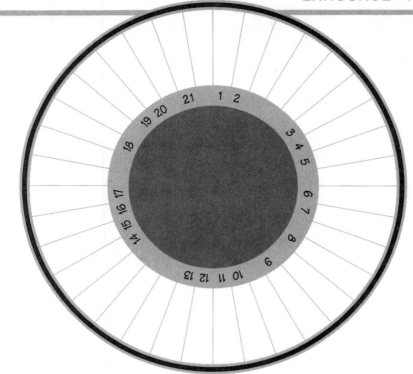

CLUES

1. Wedge
2. Gretsky's game
3. Orb
4. Bakery must
5. Spring festival
6. Cubic meter
7. Shipworm
8. Decorate again

9. Finished
10. FDR's ___ Deal
11. Female sheep
12. United
13. Revises
14. Upperclass-
     man (abbr.)
15. Grain

16. Burglar
17. Omelet must
18. Mast rope
19. Affirmative
20. Affirmative
21. ___ as (for
     example)

HINT: 16 is YEGG.

Twisted Terminology

DIRECTIONS

Arguments begin when one word leads to another, and in this puzzle words not only lead to each other, but often overlap. If you start in slot #1 with the right word and continue clockwise you should have little trouble completing the circle with 18 additional words. Each word starts in a numbered slot that corresponds to the number of the clue.

CLUES

1. The ____ (vigorous dance)
2. Peninsula
3. Rumple
4. But (Lat.)
5. Move sideways
6. Offspring; obtain
7. Characteristic attitudes
8. Not these
9. Sprayed
10. Movie : Oscar ::
    Mystery novel : ___

11. En ____
12. Passionate
13. Fender mishap
14. A Roosevelt
15. Swirl
16. Color
17. ___ man (servile sycophant)
18. Inflamed swelling
19. Still

Answer on page 219

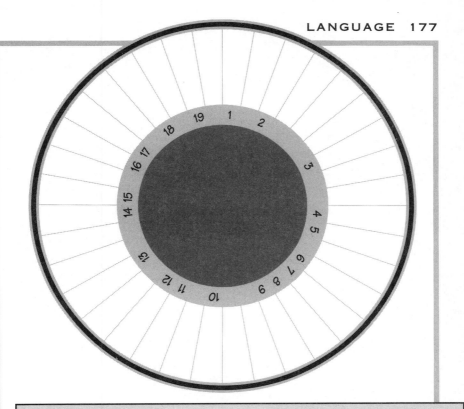

Didjaknow...
STRANGE SYMBOLS PROCESSED IN RIGHT BRAIN

Since language is generally processed in the left hemisphere, this side of the brain becomes quick and proficient at understanding data containing printed words. The right hemisphere is not programmed as well for language — it processes a word slowly, letter by letter. However, when the typeface or word shapes are *not* familiar, this slow, right brain method of processing is actually a better system for decoding data.

HINT: 7 is ETHOS.

DIRECTIONS

Arguments begin when one word leads to another, and in this puzzle words not only lead to each other, but often overlap. If you start in slot #1 with the right word and continue clockwise you should have little trouble completing the circle with 18 additional words. Each word starts in a numbered slot that corresponds to the number of the clue.

CLUES

1. Elm, e.g.
2. Marsh plant
3. Redact
4. Tizzy
5. George Michael Cohan's "Over ____"
6. Well-____ (quite knowledgeable)
7. Find the sum
8. Between cube and mince
9. Building material
10. Make a beginning (upon)
11. Brief and pithy
12. Flow gradually
13. Impressively great
14. Ancient of northern Britain
15. Rhythmical stress
16. Employ
17. Char
18. Is for many
19. Soak

Answer on page 219

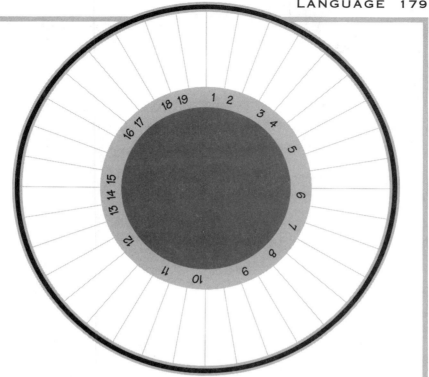

Didjaknow... LEFT-HANDERS CAN RECOVER LANGUAGE MORE RAPIDLY

After a stroke left-handers often recover language abilities quicker than right-handed women and men, even if those lefties also process language dominantly in their left hemispheres. Left-handers can more easily activate their right-brain processing centers if left-brain language centers are damaged by, for example, a stroke or severe blow. Women normally use both hemispheres anyway, certainly more than men do.

HINT: 15 *is* ICTUS.

Jam Session

DIRECTIONS

Arguments begin when one word leads to another, and in this puzzle words not only lead to each other, but often overlap. If you start in slot #1 with the right word and continue clockwise you should have little trouble completing the circle with 17 additional words. Each word starts in a numbered slot that corresponds to the number of the clue.

Didjaknow... **DECLARATIVE MEMORY REFERS TO FACTS**

The word "memory" commonly refers to conscious, *declarative* memory which involves information and events that are learned, such as

remembering what you did last week, the names of our last six presidents or answers to crossword puzzle clues. Areas of the brain essential for processing this type of memory for words include the hippocampus, amygdala, and cortex surrounding the inner surfaces of the temporal lobe located just above the left ear. *Non-declarative* memory, such as learned abilities, including skills and habits, is processed in other brain centers.

Answer on page 219

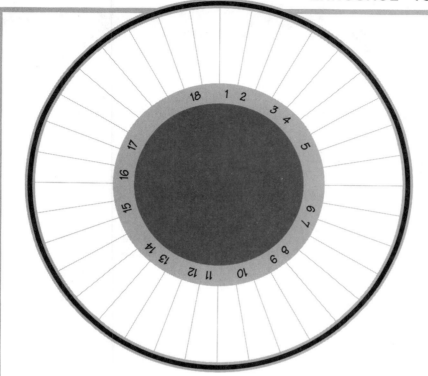

CLUES

1. Fruit preserve
2. Fossil resin
3. European capital
4. Actor Borgnine
5. Cuddle
6. Conducted
7. Rim
8. Precious stone
9. Ant (dial.)
10. Paris subway
11. Between walk and run
12. Helicopter part
13. Pulled apart
14. Excessively adorned
15. Ancient Egyptian deity
16. Flag
17. ___ off (went off the air)
18. ___ vu

HINT: 9 is EMMET.

Hang In There!

DIRECTIONS

This puzzle combines anagrams and word hunts. Write out the letters corresponding to the numbers (A=1, B=2, etc.), then rearrange the letters to make a new word that fits the clue. Fill in each square in the grid with its corresponding number and find and circle each of the answers in the grid. Some words are diagonal, and some read from right to left or bottom to top. The first definition is done for you.

CLUES

A. 1 12 7 12 15 23 19   Capone shines scaffold
AL GLOWS/GALLOWS

B. 7 18 1 9 12 13 15 20 8   Insect on knightly quest finds mathematical exponent

C. 14 5 1 20 13 1 9 4   Tidy hired help was lively

D. 12 5 1 4   Metal for trade

E. 20 18 1 9 20   Characteristic of singer John

F. 1 23 18 25   Wrong to be cautious

G. 4 21 14 5 19   Sahara sights uncovered objects

H. 20 9 5 7 1 12   Even girl can use a bandage

I. 4 21 1 12   Twofold praise

J. 18 5 1 12 12 19 20   Sincere Navy craft is starlike

K. 19 5 1 18 20 15 5   Optimistic after hot foot

L. 13 15 18 5 22 9 16   Sir Thomas Big Shot will get better

M. 19 5 14 19 9 20 9 22 5   Touchy when social call was sighted (two words)

N. 20 1 13 5 4 18 15 3   Subdued fabulous bird and formed military group (two words)

Answer on page 220

14	5	5	19	20	9	19	9	22	14
19	20	5	12	12	1	18	4	5	13
20	1	5	2	20	18	5	1	8	14
15	5	20	23	21	20	18	20	19	21
4	19	1	4	1	16	9	14	5	4
5	15	7	13	21	18	7	1	1	5
22	18	9	2	1	1	25	5	18	19
18	14	12	7 G	1 A	12 L	12 L	15 O	23 W	19 S
1	9	15	5	22	15	18	16	13	9
3	12	13	1	14	5	18	15	20	3

O. 18 5 16 21 2 12 9 3 1 14   Elephantine politico close by the community at large (two words)

P. 9 14 4 5 16   ____endence Day languished?

Q. 13 5 4   Resort club becomes abbreviated party

R. 3 1 22 15 18 20 5 4   Leaped about first, then slice Dorothy (two words)

S. 25 5 1   Indeed yes!

HINT: E is RAITT.

Sheep Speak

DIRECTIONS

This puzzle combines anagrams and word hunts. Write out the letters corresponding to the numbers (A=1, B=2, etc.), then rearrange the letters to make a new word that fits the clue. Fill in each square in the grid with its corresponding number and find and circle each of the answers in the grid. Some words are diagonal, and some read from right to left or bottom to top.

CLUES

A. 19 20 1 2 12 5 — Manger site produces farm noises

B. 19 20 1 7 8 15 18 14 — Male deer plus antler made spook split (two words)

C. 20 9 14 1 21 4 9 15 — Metal sound gets tryout

D. 14 15 20 9 1 14 — 'Tisn't Scottish John, 'tis tribe

E. 1 14 14 1 13 5 19 19 — Magnani untidiness leads to sound mind (two words, Lat.)

F. 8 5 9 7 8 20 19 — Hills and Everest, comparatively speaking

G. 20 1 18 7 5 20 19 — Goals for filmmaker: go after Julia Roberts type (two words)

H. 3 1 18 8 9 14 7 5 — Auto door necessity to arrive at card game finale (two words)

I. 1 12 15 14 7 18 5 19 20 — Simmered down after an extended interval of silence (two words)

J. 5 18 9 3 1 19 20 15 4 — Jong's digit is a matter understood by few

K. 1 12 9 5 14 — Foreign dress style (hyph.)

L. 6 18 5 5 23 8 5 5 12 19 — Coasts along with comparatively less cads (two words)

M. 19 20 1 18 — Preeminent Peter the Great

Answer on page 220

6	13	14	1	18	20	19	15	8	7
16	5	19	15	20	5	18	9	3	1
7	14	23	20	9	8	7	14	15	1
5	19	5	5	2	9	9	10	12	21
20	19	14	23	18	7	14	9	19	4
19	1	9	20	8	8	14	7	20	20
20	14	19	3	20	5	5	15	1	9
1	1	1	15	21	19	18	5	5	15
18	5	7	14	1	20	19	15	12	14
18	14	15	9	20	1	14	7	2	19

N. 23 9 14 5 19   Clarets give you strength

O. 19 9 14 14 5 18   Wrongdoer lands some shots next to the bull's-eye

P. 1 20 20 21   Aleutian island gets tense

Q. 20 15 18 20   Legally wrong pace

R. 9 19 8 20 1   Divine form states archaically

HINT: J is ESOTERICA

CITATIONS:

P. 138 American Stroke Association (2000)

P. 140, 150 Denckla, Martha Bridge, MD, Director, Developmental Cognitive Neurology, The Johns Hopkins School of Medicine. From a Presentation at Science of Cognition Conference, Library of Congress, Washington, D.C., 6 Oct. 1999.

P. 142, 154 Stromswold, K. et al. (1996). Localization of syntactic comprehension by Positron Emission Tomography. Brain and Language 52:452-73; Snowden, D. S. et al. (1996). Linguistic ability in early life and cognitive function and Alzheimer's disease in late life. Journal of the American Medical Association 275/7:528-32.

P. 144, 146 Eden, Guinevere D. Phil., Georgetown University Medical Center. From a presentation at Science of Cognition Conference, Library of Congress, Washington, D.C., 6 Oct. 1999.

P. 148, 152, 164, 166, 168, 172, 177, 179 (2001) The Brainwaves Center, Bass River, MA.

P. 156 Goel, Vinod and Dolan, Raymond J., The functional anatomy of humor: segregating cognitive and affective components.

P. 158 Bookheimer, S.Y., et al. (2000). Patterns of Brain Activation in People at Risk for Alzheimer's Disease. New England Journal of Medicine 8/17. 343: 450-56.

P. 160 Schiller, Niels O., et al. (2001). Serial order effects in spelling errors: evidence from two dysgraphic patients. Neurocase 7: 1-14.

P. 162 Tainturier, Marie-Josephe, et al. (2001). Superior written over spoken picture naming in a case of frontotemporal dementia. Neurocase 7: 89-96.

P. 170 Petersen, Steven E. PhD., Professor, Department of Neurology and Neurological Surgery, Washington University School of Medicine. From a presentation at Science of Cognition Conference, Library of Congress, Washington, D.C., 6 Oct. 1999.

P. 174 St. George-Hyslop, Peter. (2001). University of Toronto. Nature

P. 180 Squire, Larry R. PhD, Research Career Scientist, VA Medical Center, San Diego; Professor of Psychiatry and Neuroscience, University of California-San Diego School of Medicine. From a Presentation at the Science of Cognition Conference, Library of Congress, Washington, D. C., 6 Oct. 1999.

Section Six
SOCIAL-EMOTIONAL

Consciousness in humans is awareness of emotions. Emotions are the exposed tips of responses to sub-conscious survival-needs that our primitive brain systems pick up — immediate danger, opportunities to reproduce, sources of food. Humans can become consciously aware of some of their body's automatic reactions set in motion by unconscious responses to basic survival stimuli. The human animal may be unique in its ability to see itself as a player in the primitive drama of survival. It can then control its emotional reactions, sometimes, with an eye to future benefit. In his book "The Feeling of What Happens," Antonio R. Damasio calls that self-awareness "consciousness." The title draws a line in the sand. On one side stands the neuroscientific study of the human nervous system as it alerts and signals and responds body-wide. On the other, stands the philosophical or religious approach to human consciousness which tends to attribute something *that* uniquely influential to a specific organ or ephemeral beyond the biological realm.

When the brain becomes aware of any passing data it considers to be "survival-quality," it releases hormones and neurotransmitters that cause increased heart rate, eye dilation, trembling, goose bumps, and many other physical changes we are, and are not, conscious of. What self-awareness there is takes place in the cortex, mostly the front part over the eyes, an area that allows humans to plan ahead and cooperate in social groups. The gift of the frontal part of the human cortex is awareness of how the more primitive part of the brain is responding. That awareness allows humans to control their primitive responses for long-term benefit without sacrificing short-term safety. Don't worry, if the danger is imminently life-threatening, the cortex never hears about it;

the primitive brain systems freeze you or start you running without your even being aware of anything. The brain needs only nanoseconds to transmit a signal, such as "tyrannosaurus rex there," from the primitive limbic system to the cortex, and wait while the cortex checks past experience to make sure it is not just a cloud formation so you can go on picking bananas before it is too dark. Even so, the limbic system reacts first and leaves the thinking until later on the principal that if you stop to remember the name of something as big as a "Tyrannosaurus" it is too late. Yes, emotions can get humans into trouble — from constant stress responses to a bad marriage — but survival has always been the tradeoff.

The human cortex's role in restricting the expression of emotions allows people to get along with each other, for one thing. They can then achieve long-term goals that allow them to survive. Thanks to self-awareness, individuals can choose to put limitations on their personal advantage for the protection they reap from long-term social support. Perhaps guilt is the downside of that "gift" of self-awareness. On the other hand, remorseless sociopaths often turn out to have suffered damage to the same part of the prefrontal cortex that controls emotions in favor of the future fruits of social cooperation.

We find it difficult to devise pencil-on-paper exercises for such subject matter. Appropriate emotional response and effective social interaction present moving targets that true-false and multiple choice cannot hit. This Section, therefore, offers mental exercises that two people can do together. It provides scientific findings about gender differences in the human brain and it offers self-tests, one of which asks you to compare your ethics with those of business school grads and convicted felons.

DIRECTIONS

This one will be more fun if you work on it with another person. It presents two interesting challenges. The first part will show bias in how you think. The second will test your ability to recognize social needs and accurately link images with the appropriate need.

The symbols on the facing page were designed for the Olympic Games. Your first challenge is to pair each symbol with one other symbol in ways you find most compellingly significant. There is no "correct" solution, but how you choose to pair them will reveal whether your dominant skill is convergent, inside-the-envelope logic or divergent, outside-the-envelope creative flexibility.

Your second challenge is to identify the message each symbol was originally designed to deliver as used in the venue of the Olympic Games. Try to come up with only one-or two-word answers. If you are design-savvy or an Olympic sports aficionado, see how close you can come to naming the host nation for which these were designed and the year they were used. There are correct answers to the the two parts of this second challenge.

Didjaknow... INFANTS ARE AMBIDEXTROUS

All newborns will reach for a reward with the nearest hand. Even if an infant usually grabs with her right hand, if you place an object left of midline, she will grab with her left. Even if her left hand is restrained, she still will not reach with her far right hand. This is normal infant behavior. It does not mean your child will grow up to be ambidextrous. Only after a child begins walking, can a parent conclude whether a child is left- or right-handed.

Answer on page 220

HINT: The icons in the bottom row represent four separate Olympic sports.

Possible Pairs

DIRECTIONS

Make seven pairs out of these 14 different items. Use each picture once and don't leave out any pictures. Pair them so that all seven are the best combinations, based on whatever similarities make most sense to you. There is no "correct" solution; some possibilities are given on the answer page.

For fun, try this one with a friend, and see if you both match the items in the same way. Score two points for each pair of yours that matches your friend's answer, and zero points for each pair that doesn't match. Twelve to 14 points: like minds. Eight to 10 points: keep talking. Zero to six points: different planets.

Didjaknow... EXPRESSING EMOTION IS A UNIVERSAL COMMUNICATION

Did you know that animals and humans are alike in the way they express some emotions? Dogs, apes and humans all show anger and aggression in the same way: the exact same muscles move and the face looks the same in its major features. You will certainly understand if a dog makes an angry face at you, and a dog will know if you make an angry face at him. This universal display and interpretation of anger is a physical form of communication that has evolved, yet still exists between species because it is important for survival.

Answer on page 220

HINT: Go with your first impressions. Then turn the page upside down and pair them again.

In a recent study, inmates in three minimum-security prisons were presented with the ethical issues contained in the questions that follow. The same questions were posed to students in business programs at a dozen universities. The answer section compares the way MBA students and inmates responded. How do your answers compare with the responses of the two groups?

Mr. Stern is a long-time, faithful employee of your company. He works in the sales department of the computer test equipment division, where his job is to locate used test equipment that hi-tech companies are willing to part with, negotiate a price, and pass the equipment on to the engineering department for refurbishment and resale.

Mr. Stern used to be one of your company's top sales executives, but lately his productivity has been slipping. For the last two years, his monthly commissions have been lower than those of most of the younger account executives in the sales department, lower even than some of the brand-new sales employees. Part of the problem may be that at his age — 62 — Mr. Stern just might not relate very well to the young computer engineers in the hi-tech companies he's dealing with. His territory also has a fair amount of ethnic diversity, and it might not be a bad idea to add more minority members to the sales department staff. (Mr. Stern is white.) While he is still a faithful and diligent employee, the feeling among upper management is that Mr. Stern is no longer worth his base salary.

What would you do if you were told by your superior to pressure Mr. Stern into early retirement in order to:

Answer on page 221

i. make room for a younger employee
ii. make room for a member of a minority race, or
iii. save the firm the cost of full benefits

i.
(A) Just do it.

(B) Object, but still do it.

(C) Transfer or demote the employee, but don't fire him.

(D) Suggest early retirement to the employee, but don't pressure him.

(E) Just not do it — it's not right.

(F) Just not do it — it's not my job, or there might be legal problems.

ii.
(A) Just do it.

(B) Object, but still do it.

(C) Transfer or demote the employee, but don't fire him.

(D) Suggest early retirement to the employee, but don't pressure him.

(E) Just not do it — it's not right.

(F) Just not do it — it's not my job, or there might be legal problems..

iii.
(A) Just do it.

(B) Object, but still do it.

(C) Transfer or demote the employee, but don't fire him.

(D) Suggest early retirement to the employee, but don't pressure him.

(E) Just not do it — it's not right.

(F) Just not do it — it's not my job, or there might be legal problems.

Reading Faces

The ability to perceive the emotions signaled by facial expressions is a social necessity. The ability to read negative expressions (anger or disgust) begins to deteriorate in the later stages of dementia.

Of these four sets of eyes, only one is a smile of sincere, spontaneous joy. Of the others, one belongs with a neutral expression, one with condescension and one with anger. Which is which?

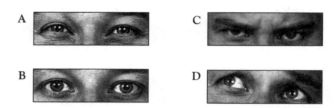

On the opposite page the full faces are revealed down the right-hand side of the page. Only one configuration of the muscles creates the *Duchenne smile* (a smile of sincere, spontaneous joy). The difference is in the use of the orbicularis oculi muscle around the eye (see illustration at right), which is the only reliable indicator of sincere joy. Do the smiling mouths on the faces down the right-hand side of the opposite page change the way you perceive the true emotion expressed?

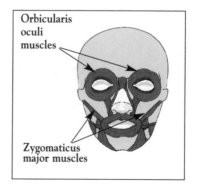

Orbicularis oculi muscles

Zygomaticus major muscles

Duchenne
smiling face

Angry face

Neutral face

Condescending face

You can make yourself feel happier by smiling — as long as you make the right *kind* of smile! Also, you can tell a sincere smile from a false smile — and, in some cases, tell an honest person from a liar — by paying attention to the muscle around the eye.

People–Power

DIRECTIONS

Your memory perks up when emotions are involved because the brain, which is designed to keep you alive, is equipped with sensors alert for incoming data that relate to food, sex and danger. That is one reason people are usually more interested in other people than mere facts about things. Equally important, if a new piece of data relates somehow to something already known, it is easier to remember.

On the opposite page there are two groups of statements, one of which is upside down. (Don't look at that one yet.) Read the rightside-up list.

Now cover that page and try to answer these questions without looking.

Who wore a blue dress?

Who had a small moustache?

Who painted sunflowers?

Who tried to overcome a problem?

Who won a court judgement?

Whose husband died?

Turn the book upside-down and read the other list of sentences. Cover the page and try the same questions again. Did you get more right this time? Why?

Kerry looked good in a blue dress.

Allen had a small moustache.

Mac painted some sunflowers.

Wally devoted his life to overcoming a social injustice.

David won a crucial Supreme Court judgment.

Betty's husband died tragically.

Didjaknow... INFANTS CAN'T HELP BEING CONTRARY

Your infant or toddler is not being willfully naughty when she says "No" out loud while she continues to throw toys out of the playpen. Even though baby may want to please you, cognitive brain development has not matured enough to inhibit actions that provided a reward in the past. This is why you will often see a baby making an incorrect choice or action, even when she knows and can say what the correct choice is. With time, baby will learn to inhibit impulses and unite knowledge, choices and behavior.

Monica looked good in a blue dress.

Adolf had a small moustache.

Vincent painted some sunflowers.

Martin devoted his life to overcoming a social injustice.

George won a crucial Supreme Court judgment.

Jacqueline's husband died tragically.

People who are most likely to create false memories in response to misinformation tend to score higher in tests that rate their ability to produce vivid visual imagery on demand, are likely to be hypnotized more easily and to show a greater need for social approval.

For this self-test, you will need a helper to play the role of "hypnotist" by slowly reading the following segments of text aloud as you concentrate with your eyes closed on what you hear.

PART ONE — Read this aloud:

"For this first part, please close your eyes and sit in a relaxed position. Place your left hand in your lap with the palm facing up.

"Imagine that Novocaine is being injected into the little finger of your left hand. You feel the slight prick of the needle in the tip of your little finger and then your finger starts to tingle the same as when you sleep on your arm or when some part of your body falls asleep. You feel your little finger tingle, and then you feel the very tip start to go numb. Imagine the Novocaine moving up your finger, as first the tip goes numb, and then the first knuckle, and then the second knuckle, and then your whole little finger is numb all the way to where it meets your hand. Now, the whole little finger on your left hand is completely numb, like a fat lump of clay.

"Now imagine the Novocaine moving into your next finger, the ring finger, as it starts to feel numb as well. Tell yourself that this next finger is feeling number and number, until it too feels like a lump of clay, or a fat piece of rubber. Now, both fingers are numb, fat, and rubbery.

"Now, bend your thumb over and feel the two fingers at the other end of your hand. Those fingers are so numb that they can't really feel the thumb touching them, just a dull sensation of pressure.

"Now, tell yourself you've just imagined the whole thing, and your fingers feel perfectly normal, and not numb at all, and you can feel sensations in them perfectly fine."

PART TWO

"For this part, lie down. Keep your eyes closed as you listen to the instructions.

"Imagine yourself lying by a lake in Northern Italy. There's a carpet of warm, fragrant grass beneath you. It's a beautiful summer day, with a warm sun shining out of a robin's-egg-blue sky. A gentle breeze caresses your face. Picture the blue sky with a few small, cottony clouds floating slowly by, and feel the warm sun on your face and neck. In the distance you hear a small child laugh.

"Feel the gentle warmth of the sun soothe your shoulders and chest as you lie on the soft grass. The breeze caresses the backs of your hands, and then you notice how warm and pleasant the sun feels on them. Your shoulders, arms, and hands feel so relaxed in the warm sun and gentle breeze. Small, brightly-colored sailboats drift lazily on the blue lake.

"Tell yourself that you've never felt so relaxed, as the warmth of the sun flows down your arm and through your fingers, down your chest to your stomach and legs. Just let yourself go limp. The smell of the warm grass is so relaxing, so soothing. Let yourself feel the warmth of the sun as every muscle in your body melts into complete relaxation. Even your toes feel warm, calm, at peace with the grass, the water lapping at the lake's shore, the blue sky, the universe. Just let yourself feel calm, relaxed, so lazy you might never get up.

"Now, open your eyes and let yourself continue to feel relaxed, but awake and alert at the same time. You may get up if you wish."

Didjaknow... YOU'LL HAVE AN EDGE IF YOU STAND TO HIS LEFT IN A FACE-TO-FACE

Next time your boss calls you into his office to debate a work issue, try sitting or standing to the left side of him. Being in his left visual field forces your boss's brain to use its right side first, before passing it over to his left hemisphere where language is normally processed. Why would this give you an edge? For most people, the hemisphere on the right side of the brain is literal — more likely to take action than compare incoming data with past experience. Therefore your boss's first impression is less likely to be analytical and so it will be less judgmental. Remember, in face-to-face confrontation, move to the left of the person you are going up against.

SCORING:

1. In the first part, you were asked to imagine that first your little finger and then the second finger on your left hand were turning numb from a shot of Novocaine. Compared to what you would have felt if your finger really had been injected with Novocaine, what you felt was:

> Not at all the same (0 pt.)
> A little the same (1 pt.)
> Somewhat the same (2 pts.)
> Much the same (3 pts.)
> Exactly the same (4 pts.)

2. In the second part, you were asked to imagine that you were lying by a peaceful Italian lake, with a warm sun and gentle breeze making you feel completely relaxed. Compared to what you would have felt if you really had been relaxing by an Italian lake, what you felt was:

> Not at all the same (0 pt.)
> A little the same (1 pt.)
> Somewhat the same (2 pts.)
> Much the same (3 pts.)
> Exactly the same (4 pts.)

Totals: 0-3 pts.: Low hypnotizability
4-6 pts.: Average hypnotizability
7-8 pts.: High hypnotizability

ANATOMICAL DIFFERENCES

The human brain is composed of three major components: gray matter, where computation takes place, consists of nerve cells, dendrites, and axons; white matter, called myelin, that acts like insulation for the "wires" that gray matter uses to communicate from one region to another; and cerebrospinal fluid. While females have a smaller cranium than males (1200cc versus 1400cc), they have the same amount of gray matter as men. As cranial volume increases, men show a proportionate increase in gray and white matter, but women show a disproportionate increase: 50% of a male brain is gray matter, but 55% of the female brain will be gray matter. Why? Because woman's smaller cranium adapts by packing more neurons into it and, because there is less space, less white matter is needed to protect the "wires" since the neurons have a shorter distance to travel.

DIFFERENCES IN RESPONSE TIME

It is common knowledge that men tend to be physically bigger than women, but males also have the ability to execute motor commands quicker and more accurately than females. When asked to tap a finger during a battery of motor function tests, it was found that men could tap their fingers much faster than women. A light beam measured the tapping to ensure the difference had nothing to do with muscle strength. Moreover, PET scan studies show the cerebellum is more active in men and, since this is the area of the brain having to do with motor skills, it helps explain why men excel on tests involving motor function.

DIFFERENCE IN FOCUS

Male and female brains were studied by FMRI (function magnetic resonance imaging) while performing spatial and language tests. For both sexes, the imaging revealed a greater increase of activity in the left hemisphere for verbal problems, relative to greater increase in the right hemisphere for spatial tasks. Women appear to recruit both sides of the brain for both tasks, i.e., their brains literally race all over the place to recall an answer. This may be an advantage for some tasks. As verbal tests get harder, more regions need to be searched to find the answer. But using both hemispheres puts women at a disadvantage for spatial tasks. Because one part (the right hemisphere) of men's brains is specialized to perform spatial tasks, they perform better for that reason than women who lack a specialized area for spatial processing.

WOMEN REMEMBER VISUAL DETAILS BETTER

If you want the real lowdown on what the Jones's house looks like, it's best to ask a woman because recent tests show that women exhibit a greater visual memory than men. A group of men and women were asked to carefully study a picture of a roomful of furniture for one minute. They were then given a picture of an empty room and shown various pieces of furniture. Asked if various pieces of furniture had been in the room and, if so, where they had been situated, women remembered the items and where they were placed much better than men.

DIFFERENCES IN CONTROLLING EMOTIONAL IMPULSES

After the age of 40, men begin to lose that part of the brain that says, "Stop and think about the consequences!" Besides being responsible for abstraction, mental flexibility and attention, the frontal lobe also plays the role of the inhibiter. It is intimately connected to the limbic system, which is the emotional part of the brain, but the relationship between the two is reciprocal. While the emotional part of the brain may say, "Let's, do it," the frontal part will respond: "Wait! Think of the outcome!" Young men have larger frontal lobes than women, proportionate to body size, but after the age of 40, a man's frontal lobe will begin to shrink. A woman's frontal lobe, however, does not shrink with age.

BOTH MEN AND WOMEN HAVE TWO EMOTIONAL BRAINS...

The emotional or limbic brain can be divided into two subsystems located deep within the center of the brain: the limbic system and, below that, the "older" reptilian response system. This old limbic system reacts to emotion through action, and because evolution does not throw anything away, this part still exists deep in the human brain. The second part of the emotional brain lies above it, in the cingulate gyrus of the cortex. The cingulate gyrus is new in evolutionary terms and evolved along with the brain's vocal and language areas. The new limbic system provides ways to modulate emotion by expressing it through language, making humans the only species on earth who can both act out and verbalize emotion.

...BUT THE "OLD" LIMBIC BRAIN IS MORE ACTIVE IN MEN

There's a big difference in the way men and women handle emotion, and this is especially true when they become angry. Read any newspaper and it becomes obvious that when it comes to acts of violence and aggression, men win hands down. The likelihood that a murder is committed by a man is 40,000:1 and this phenomenon is seen all over the world. It's not due to physical strength alone — firearms equalize this factor since it doesn't takes much strength to pull a trigger. While men may show anger in an aggressive, physical manner, women tend to be verbal. Men fight. Women talk it over.

EMOTIONS ARE KEY TO SURVIVAL FOR BOTH MEN AND WOMEN

There are six emotions that can be reliably detected on the human face in every culture around the world — and detecting emotion in others is a key element in the survival game. The six emotions are anger, fear, sadness, disgust, surprise and happiness. Lower species, such as crocodiles and rats, do not smile. Therefore, happiness or a sense of humor is recognized as a fairly new emotion in the evolutionary scale. Happiness is the only positive emotion displayed on the human face; no other is seen. Because the evolutionary process has shown that it is more important for the survival of a species to show negative emotions, this will explain why humans display five negative emotions and only one positive.

WOMEN ARE QUICKER AND MORE ACCURATE AT DETECTING EMOTIONS

When a face is computer-morphed into the shape of vase, a woman can tell whether it is happy or sad in 30 milliseconds. It will take her 20 milliseconds more to decide whether the image is a face or a vase. Men, on the other hand, take longer to attach an emotion to the image. Moreover, PET scan studies have shown that women did not have to activate much of their brain to gauge the correct facial emotion. And even though a man takes longer, and activates more of his brain to identify an emotion, he is still less likely to come up with the correct answer.

FEAR IS AN EMOTION MUCH MORE EASILY DETECTED BY WOMEN

There is a dramatic difference in the way men and women detect the facial expression of fear. And when men feel real fear, rather than posing with a fearful expression, women can detect the truly felt emotion much more easily. Men had a harder time identifying fear in other men, even when the man observed was actually feeling fear. And when a woman is the one expressing fear, the same result is even greater: men have a much harder time differentiating a woman's truly evoked fear from a posed fear.

MEN CAN TELL WHEN A WOMAN IS HAPPY MUCH MORE EASILY THAN WHEN SHE IS SAD

Emotional discrimination tests given to groups of men and women showed one striking similarity: Women are more sensitive to happy and sad emotions expressed on the faces of men than of women. Men are also more sensitive to emotions expressed on a man's face. However, men find it more difficult to detect sadness on the faces of women. Although men are more likely to detect real sadness than a false expression of sadness, if you're a woman you cannot take it for granted that your man can always tell if you're sad just by looking at your face.

CITATIONS

P. 190 Diamond, Adele (1999). Learning and the Brain Conference, Boston, MA. November 7-9.

P. 192 Gur, Ruben C. (1999). Sex Differences in Learning. From a presentation at the Learning and the Brain Conference, Boston, MA. November 7-9.

P. 196, 197 Ekman, Paul (1992). Facial expressions of emotion: new findings, new questions. Psychological Science 3/1:34-8.
Ekman, Paul et al (1988). Smiles when lying. Journal of Personality and Social Psychology 54/3:414-20.

P. 200 Drake, R.A. and Binghamm, B.R. (1985). Induced lateral orientation and persuasibility. Brain Cognition 4:156-64.
Drake, R. A. (1991). Processing persuasive arguments: recall and recognition as a function of agreement and manipulated activation asymmetry. Brain Cognition 15/1:83-94.

P. 202-209 Gur, Rubin C.

Solutions

SECTION ONE: EXECUTIVE

```
  4 + 8 + 9 = 21
  5 + 7 + 9 = 21
  6 + 7 + 8 = 21
3 + 9 + 8 + 1 = 21
2 + 7 + 3 + 9 = 21
3 + 4 + 9 + 5 = 21
7 + 5 + 3 + 6 = 21
```

GAMBLER'S CHOICE P. 14

	2	1	+	3	6	=	5	7
		9	x	6	+	3	=	5	7
		8	x	8	-	7	=	5	7
	9	x	8	-	1	5	=	5	7
	2	9	x	2	-	1	=	5	7
4	4	+	1	8	-	5	=	5	7

ANGRY*!$%?TYPIST P. 16

15	6	9	4
10	3	16	5
8	13	2	11
1	12	7	14

THIRTY-FOUR ALL P. 18

```
 2 4 3     3 8 1     1 5 4
+6 7 5    +5 4 6    +7 8 2
-------   -------   -------
 9 1 8     9 2 7     9 3 6

 3 2 7     2 3 8     2 4 5
+6 1 8    +7 1 6    +7 1 8
-------   -------   -------
 9 4 5     9 5 4     9 6 3

 3 5 4     2 4 6
+6 1 8    +7 3 5
-------   -------
 9 7 2     9 8 1
```

MAGIC NINES P. 20

1	9	6	1	4
3	6	1	1	9
2	8	9	1	7
2	5	6	1	6
3	2	4	1	8

In each horizontal row, the three-digit number at the left is the square of the two-digit number at the right. The square root of 324 is 18.

THE SQUARE ROOTER P. 22

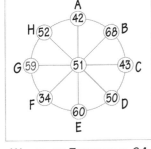

WHEEL OF FORTUNE P. 24

October and November of a year in which October first falls on a Tuesday.

S	M	T	W	T	F	S
		1			4	
		8	9		11	12
		22			25	
	28	29	30			
	4				8	

FOWL PLAY P. 26

```
⚁ + ⚃ = ⚀          3/5 + 2/5 = 1
⚅ = ⚅              6/3 = 2
⚁ + ⚀ = ⚂          1 + 2 = 3
⚄ = ⚄              10/2 = 5
⚅ + ⚂ = ⚅          6/2 + 3/1 = 6
⚅ + ⚂ = ⚅          5/1 + 4 = 9
⚄ + ⚄ = ⚄          6 + 4 = 10
⚅ + ⚄ = ⚅          6/1 + 5 = 11
```

DOMI-ROWS P. 28

```
              1
              E
      2      2
 1   E   E   1
  E     V     E
      A
 2   E   V   E 2
              E
              1
```

At each extreme of the diamond only one EVA can be made for a total of four. On each side two Es touch one V for a total of eight EVEs.

ADAM & EVA? P. 30

The only positive, one-possibility statement was Dick's.
The others were guessing.

ABLE ACCOUNTANT P. 32

In each horizontal row, the numbers in column C equal half the difference between the numbers in columns A and B. Thus the missing number is half of 364, or 182.

	A	B	C
	108	356	124
	196	780	292
	284	648	182

MIDDLE C'S P. 34

3	9	4	7	8
8	1	5	2	3
7	8	3	6	5
6	5	7	4	1
4	3	2	5	9

FIVES ARE WILD P. 36

(13)	(1)	(6)	(10)
(14)	(2)	(5)	(9)
	(12)	(11)	(7)
(3)	(15)	(8)	(4)

CHANGING PLACES P. 38

ASTRO-LOGICAL P. 40

SECTION TWO: MEMORY

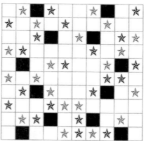

EARLY EARLY BIRD P. 46

13				⁴X	13
			³÷	¹¹+	
		⁴−	¹⁷X		
	⁵÷	⁷+			
¹²³+	⁸−				
⁶−					
=\n181					

LUCKY THIRTEEN P. 48

Theme Word:
SPORTS

1. Severiano Ballesteros
2. Cassius Clay
3. Edson Pele
4. Denis Potvin
5. Richard Petty
6. Nancy Lopez
7. Walter Payton
8. Mark Spitz
9. Bjorn Borg
10. Evonne Goolagong
11. Eddie Arcaro
12. Maurice Richard
13. Jim Brown
14. Ted Williams
15. George Brett
16. Katarina Witt
17. Barry Sanders
18. Boris Spassky

GREAT SCOTT! P. 50

Theme Word:
DRAMA

1. Phyllis Diller
2. Doris Day
3. Danny DeVito
4. Robert Redford
5. Al Hirt
6. Muhammad Ali
7. Arthur Ashe
8. Dom DiMaggio Joe DiMaggio Vince DiMaggio
9. Milton Berle
10. Agatha Christie
11. Desi Arnaz

THAT'S ENTERTAINMENT P. 52

Theme Word: MUSIC

1. Miles Davis
2. Mary Martin
3. Martha Graham
4. Thelonious Monk
5. Franz Schubert
6. Claude Debussy
7. Johann Strauss
8. Roger Sessions
9. Jasha Heifetz
10. Leonard Bernstein
11. Gioacchino Rossini
12. Enrico Caruso
13. Hoagy Carmichael
14. Aaron Copland

HEAVENLY HARMONIES P. 54

Theme Words P. 50 -54

S	S	S	S	S	S
P	P	P	P	P	P
O	O	O	O	O	O
R	R	R	R	R	R
T	T	T	T	T	T
S	S	S	S	S	S

D	D	D	D	D
R	R	R	R	R
A	A	A	A	A
M	M	M	M	M
A	A	A	A	A

M	M	M	M	M
U	U	U	U	U
S	S	S	S	S
I	I	I	I	I
C	C	C	C	C

FRENCH CONNECTION P. 56

STARS & STRIPES P. 58

BIRTH OF A NATION P. 60

DIGIT-TALLIES P. 62

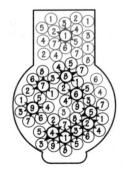

CIRCLES WITHIN CIRCLES P. 64

SECTION THREE: COMPUTATION

ADD-VENTURE PLUS P. 70

SUMMING UP P. 72

ADDENDUM & EVE? P. 74

ADDICTIVE PLEASURES P. 76

TOT UP & TALLY HO! P. 78

ADD-VANCE NOTICE P. 80

ADDS & EVENS P. 82

Start by solving 1 Across, 4 Down and 6 Down, 1 Down and 10 Across. The prime number in 8 Across is 661; the prime numbers in 9 Across are 5 and 13.

SQUARE DANCES P. 84

1 Across calls for the smallest possible odd number that will produce a two-digit square: 5. 3 Across is the three digit square of 11. 3 down gives you the beginning of 4 Across, which is then easy to complete. 5 Down and 7 Down give you all the info needed to complete the puzzle.

PRIME TIME P. 86

The entry points are 5, 7, and 8 Across, then 9 and 8 Down. The balance will come naturally.

COUNTER INTELLIGENCE P. 88

A good place to start is at 4 Across, where 9 is the only possible answer. This will lead to 2 Down and 3 Down. At 9 Across, the answer must be the cube of 5. This gives you ?-4-5 for 7 Down and ?-4-4 for 8 Across. The balance will come naturally.

CONTRIBUTING FACTORS P. 90

The consecutive numbers can't go higher than 2...6 ; this series, however, would result in 8's and would therefore be incorrect for 6 Down. 5 Across refers to a Heinz product. 8 Across is the square of 4, which in turn is the square of 2. 2 Down is the square of 16. 6 Down is the square of 25.

	1	2	3	4	5
	¹1	²2	³3	4	⁵5
■	5	7			1
⁶6	6	6	6	⁷6	
2		■	1	6	■
⁹5	4	3	2	1	

ROOT CAUSES P. 92

Begin with 5 and 8 Across, then 9 Down. For 2 Down, the first two digits could be 3-3 or7-3; the last three could be ?-1-8 or ?-1-6 depending on 6 Across. The answer to 6 Across is 81 (any other: a too-large second digit for 2 Down, which you now know begins with 7-3). This tells you that all consecutive digits are in descending order.

9	7	5	3	1
■	3	4	3	■
8	1	■	2	5
■	1	2	1	■
9	8	7	6	5

FIGURATIVELY SPEAKING P. 94

Fill in the obvious first: 1 Across, 6 Across, the first three digits of 8 Across, all of 2 Down and 3 Down. At 7 Across the largest factor of 56 is 28, half is 14, which squared gives you 7 Down. You now have completed 1 Down and you know the prime number is 41. This enables you to complete 5 Down and 10 Across.

1	7	5	1	■
6	7	6	■	1
8	1	■	1	4
1	1	1	9	4
■	1	7	6	4

CALCULATED SURPRISES P. 96

Throckmorton should begin the count at G. This is the order in which the boys leave the circle: A 13; B 9; C 5; D 10; E 11; F 1; G 2; H 7; I 3: J 8; K 6; L 4; M 12.

COUNTDOWN P. 98

Using "n" for the required number of pounds, the number of pounds times the cost per pound equals the selling price.

n oranges x 45 = 45n
20 grapefruit x 60 = 60 x 20
n + 20 mixture x 50 = 50 (n + 20)
1. 45n + 60 x 20 = 50 (n + 20)
2. 45n + 1200 = 50n + 1000
3. 200 = 5n
4. n = 40

40 pounds of oranges are needed to mix with 20 pounds of grapefruit.

APPLES & ORANGES P. 100

INVOICE

Floor Jack	$127.50
Vise	17.90
Spotlight	24.60
	$170.00

OOPS, SORRY, DICK! P. 102

A			B		
6	2	6	5	4	5
2	32	2	4	36	4
6	2	6	5	4	5

C			D		
4	6	4	3	8	3
6	40	6	8	44	8
4	6	4	3	8	3

WALL-TO-WALL BAGS P. 104

Tom had the flat tire at 2:30 p.m., after riding ten miles at 20 miles per hour, or for half an hour. Therefore he walked the remaining five miles in one hour.

A BUMP IN THE ROAD P. 106

They averaged 47 mph which is closer to 55 mph than 35 mph. Therefore they spent more time on interstate highways. The difference between the two speed limits is 20 mph Their average was 12 mph over the low speed limit and 8 mph under the high speed limit. Using this ratio, they drove 4 hours at 35 mph, or 140 miles, on local roads, and 6 hours at 55 mph, or 330 miles, on interstate highways.

WITHIN LIMITS P. 108

SECTION FOUR: SPATIAL

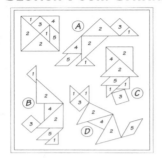

TANGRAMS P. 114

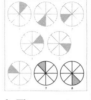

The second piece is taken directly opposite the first piece. The next piece taken is the one to the left. The next piece is opposite it; the next to the left, and so on.

A PIECE OF CAKE P. 116

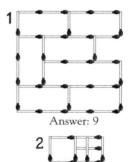

The interior design of the room and clothing of the adult parents are both made up of rectangles. The drawing their son is showing them is a curved line, implying that his values are "out of line" with theirs.

CIRCLING THE SQUARE P. 118

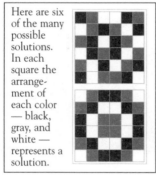

Here are six of the many possible solutions. In each square the arrangement of each color — black, gray, and white — represents a solution.

CHECKERBOARD SQUARE P. 120

ASSYRIAN MISS-TERY P. 122

1

Answer: 9

2

TWICE BURNED P. 124

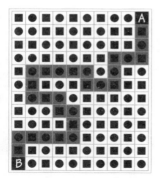

FROM A TO B P. 126

Dick knew the name of the town they had just been through, it was one of those on the signpost, and was able to orient both the sign and himself. (He also took over the driving.)

UNEXPECTED WINDFALL P. 128

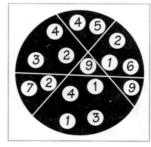

CRUNCHY CAKE P. 130

SECTION FIVE: LANGUAGE

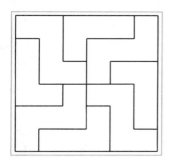

BAGS	FIX	
RAGS	FIT	SHINE
RATS	HIT	SPINE
RUTS	HOT	SPIRE
PUTS	HOP	SPARE
PITS	TOP	STARE
WITS	TOO	STORE
WITH	TWO	STONE

	SAVE	
ANY	SANE	CORNY
ANT	LANE	CORNS
AND	LINE	CORES
ADD	PINE	CORDS
ADE	PILE	CARDS
ODE	PILL	BARDS
ONE	KILL	BIRDS

TO	RULE	RODE	RID
LO	RILE	RIDE	BID
LA	BILE	SIDE	BIN
HA	BILL	SINE	TIN
HE	WILL	SANE	TON
BE	WELL	CANE	YON
BY	TELL	CANT	YOU

ART	ROPES	HOLE
ARE	HOPES	ROLE
IRE	HOPED	ROLL
IRK	LOPED	TOLL
INK	LOVED	TOOL
INS	LOVER	TOOK
ITS	COVER	BOOK

AN "L" OF A TIME P. 132   FOWL ADVICE P. 138   THOUGHTFUL BROWSING P. 140

TOE	RACE	ROBED
TOO	LACE	ROWED
WOO	LACK	SOWED
WHO	LOCK	SEWED
WHY	BOCK	SEWER
THY	BOOK	SEVER
THE	LOOK	NEVER

TIRE	LOOKS	POISE
TIME	BOOKS	NOISE
LIME	BOOTS	NOOSE
LIFE	BOOTH	MOOSE
RIFE	SOOTH	MOUSE
RIFT	SOUTH	HOUSE
GIFT	MOUTH	HORSE

ANT	SET	BURN	BUT
AND	GET	BORN	BIT
ADD	GUT	BORE	BIN
ADE	BUT	BARE	TIN
ODE	DEBT	CARE	TON
ODD	NET	CART	YON
OLD	NEW	CANT	YOU

SUN	CRAVED	HITCH
SON	BRAVED	HUTCH
TON	BRACED	HUNCH
TOE	TRACED	BUNCH
FOE	TRACES	BENCH
DOE	TRACKS	BEACH
DOG	TRICKS	TEACH

P. 138 - 145
To unscramble the sayings, order the bottom Mystery Words as follows:

P. 138 - 139: 5-2-6-1-4-3
P. 140 - 141: 5-4-3-1-8-2-6-7
P. 142 - 143: 5-4-1-6-8-2-3-7
P. 144 - 145: 5-4-8-1-2-6-3-7

GOOD HORSE SENSE P. 142   DOGGONED RIGHT! P. 144

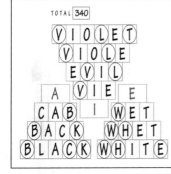

TOTAL 340

Colorful Conundrum Answer:

A			=	0
CAB	25		=	25
BACK	25 + 25		=	50
BLACK	25 + 10 + 25		=	60
				135

E			=	0
WET	15		=	15
WHET	15 + 10		=	25
WHITE	15 + 10 + 5		=	30
				70

I			=	0
VIE	25		=	25
EVIL	25 + 10		=	35
VOILE	25 + 10		=	35
VIOLET	25 + 10 + 5		=	40
				135

135
135
+ 70
Total 340

COLORFUL CONUNDRUM P. 148

WINNER-WORD P. 146

S	T	R	A	P
T	R	A	S	H
R	A	D	I	O
A	S	I	A	N
P	H	O	N	Y

WATCH PARTS P. 150

C	O	U	C	H
O	U	T	R	E
U	T	T	E	R
C	R	E	E	D
H	E	R	D	S

BIZARRE ROUTE P. 152

ERECT AN ISLAND P. 154

AGREE TO BE ANXIOUS P. 156

YALE SOUP P. 158

BARD'S HASTY DAME P. 160

REVERSED BET P. 162

DITCH THAT TRUCK! P. 164

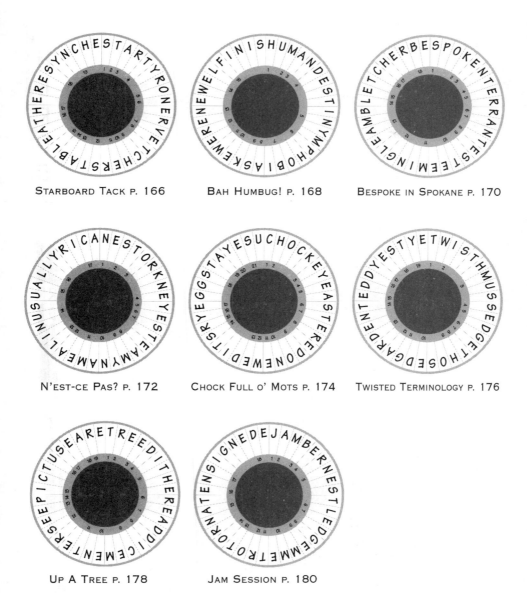

STARBOARD TACK P. 166

BAH HUMBUG! P. 168

BESPOKE IN SPOKANE P. 170

N'EST-CE PAS? P. 172

CHOCK FULL O' MOTS P. 174

TWISTED TERMINOLOGY P. 176

UP A TREE P. 178

JAM SESSION P. 180

A. AL GLOWS/GALLOWS
B. GRAIL MOTH/LOGARITHM
C. NEW MAID/ANIMATED
D. DEAL/LEAD
E. TRAIT/RAITT
F. AWRY/WARY
G. DUNES/NUDES
H. TIE GAL/LIGATE
I. DUAL/LAUD
J. REAL LST/STELLAR

K. SEAR TOE/ROSEATE
L. MORE VIP/IMPROVE
M. SENSITIVE/VISIT SEEN
N. TAMED ROC/MADE ROTC
O. REPUBLICAN/NEAR PUBLIC
P. INDEP/PINED
Q. MED/DEM
R. CAVORTED/CARVE DOT
S. YEA/AYE

HANG IN THERE! P. 182

A. STABLE/BLEATS
B. STAG HORN/GHOST RAN
C. TIN AUDIO/AUDITION
D. NOT IAN/NATION
E. ANNA MESS/MENS SANA
F. HEIGHTS/HIGHEST
G. TARGETS/GET STAR
H. CAR HINGE/REACH GIN
I. LONG REST/LOST ANGER

J. ERICA'S TOE/ESOTERICA
K. ALIEN/A-LINE
L. FREEWHEELS/FEWER HEELS
M. STAR/TSAR
N. WINES/SINEW
O. SINNER/INNERS
P. ATTU/TAUT
Q. TORT/TROT
R. ISHTA/SAITH

SHEEP SPEAK P. 184

SECTION SIX: SOCIAL/EMOTIONAL

Olympic Games, Mexico, 1968
Row 1: Telephone; Mail; Currency Exchange; First Aid
Row 2: Toilets, Men; Toilets, Women; Information; Bus
Row 3: Restaurant; Coffee Shop; Shops; No Smoking
Row 4: Smoking; Locker; Shower; Press
Row 5: Track & Field; Football; Swimming; Gymnastics

Left Brain Matches:
rain cloud — tornado
beach umbrella — sun
bugs — snail
top — noisy kids
igloo — house
bowler hat — beanie
crying lady — happy man

Right Brain Matches:
rain cloud — crying lady
beach umbrella — beanie
top — tornado
igloo — bowler hat
sun — happy man
bugs — noisy kids
snail — house

OUTSIDE THE ENVELOPE P. 190

POSSIBLE PAIRS P. 192

Answers are expressed as a percent response by MBA students and inmates respectively. Where the numbers don't add up to 100, other options such as "don't know" were chosen.

MBA Students	Inmates	MBA Students	Inmates	MBA Students	Inmates
i. (A) 22.5	(A) 46.3	ii. (A) 19.1	(A) 23.2	iii. (A) 14.9	(A) 13.6
(B) 3.0	(B) 9.1	(B) 2.8	(B) 11.7	(B) 3.4	(B) 4.5
(C) 18.6	(C) 10.6	(C) 17.5	(C) 11.1	(C) 17.0	(C) 9.1
(D) 26.4	(D) 20.3	(D) 25	(D) 31.1	(D) 20.5	(D) 31.8
(E) 15.4	(E) 4.5	(E) 19.8	(E) 13.6	(E) 25.5	(E) 25.2
(F) 7.6	(F) 4.5	(F) 8.7	(F) 4.6	(F) 9.2	(F) 11.1

DOWNSIDE OF DOWNSIZING P. 194

SECTION ONE: EXECUTIVE

"Executive" is among the most recently-evolved functions 14

Having to deal with unfamiliar data keeps brains young 16

Keeping brains sharp in retirement 18

Differences in abilities can be observed in infancy 20

Infants like to take action 22

Ability tests show gender differences 24

Females and males both mentally flexible 27

The male brain ages faster 28

Learning is hindered when the brain can't say "no" 30

Stress hormones might help or might hurt 33

Rapid response to stroke can save your life 34

Thinking increases blood flow to the brain 36

Knowledge of the world increases with age 38

Men "fight or flee"; women "tend and befriend" 40

SECTION TWO: MEMORY

Memory is the mother of all functions 46

Young brains and old brains decline at the same rate 48

Old brains use more brain 51

Infants forget when distracted 52

More brain, more memory gained 55

Long term stress hurts the hippo (and memory) 57

Musical training improves memory 59

Women are better at verbal memory 61

Early to bed makes you wise 62

The sound of language is important for comprehension 64

SECTION THREE: COMPUTATION

Use math, don't lose it 70

Counting and quantity are two different concepts 72

What parts of the brain light up when doing math in your head? 74

Left-brain damage may interfere with computation 76

Newborns perceive difference in quantities only up to 3 or 4 78

A mysterious affinity for 7's 81

Japanese words for numbers help them learn math early 82

"Chunking" helps number recall 84

Sleep deprivation leads to poor computation 87

Einstein's special genius was right-brained 89

Lefties excel at computation 91

Savants may suffer from right-brain deficit 93

Testosterone decline leads to some loss of math skills 95

Number and language skills are interdependent 97

Expert calculators use brain differently 99

Gazing to the right stimulates math skills 101

Social factors influence mental disorders 103

Body and brain differentiate stress 105

Memory improves with visualizing, 107

Boys and girls differ in the way they learn 109

SECTION FOUR: SPATIAL

Less is more for visual statement 114

Superior male spatial skills may be evolutionary 116

Sex hormones affect the brain 118

Men are better in spatial ability 120

Transsexuals have brain change 122

Men take to travel 124

Testosterone affects spatial ability 126

Exploring new avenues makes the
brain grow 129

Brain enjoys visual binding and
discovery tasks 130

Caricatures subtract and amplify 132

SECTION FIVE: LANGUAGE

Strokes in the left brain often damage
language centers 138

Learning disabilities can often be
outgrown 140

Complex sentences can confuse 142

Good reading skills are acutely acquired
and required 144

Dyslexia may be a phonological problem 146

Left brain likes familiar symbols 148

Learning disabilities are determined by
society 150

Writing test reveals left-handed thinking 152

"Like whatever" hinders teens 154

Much like chocolate and drugs 156

APOE-4 may foretell Alzheimer's 158

Misspelling may be a working memory
problem 160

"Sounds" of words not necessary for
writing? 162

Left brain usually learns language 164

Watching where the words are 166

Female brain more likely to use both
sides for language 168

Two codes are better than one 170

False words impair facts 172

Vaccine may hold hope for Alzheimer's 174

Strange symbols processed in right brain 177

Left-handers can recover language more
rapidly 179

Declarative memory refers to facts 180

SECTION SIX: SOCIAL/EMOTIONAL

Infants are ambidextrous 190

Expressing emotion is a universal
communication 192

Infants can't help being contrary 199

You'll have an edge if you stand to his
left in a face-to-face 202

Anatomical differences 204

Differences in response time 205

Difference in focus 205

Women remember visual details better 206

Differences in controlling emotional
impulses 206

Both men and women have two
emotional brains... 207

...But the "old" limbic brain is more
active in men 207

Emotions are key to survival for both
men and women 208

Women are quicker and more accurate
at detecting emotions 208

Fear is an emotion much more easily
detected by women 209

Men can tell when a woman is
happy much more easily than
when she is sad 209

Catch a New Brain Wave!

Brainwaves Books ■ 252 Great Western Road ■ South Yarmouth, MA 02664
VOICE (toll-free): 1-8778-SMARTS, ■ FAX: 508/760.2397 ■ EMAIL:<admin@brainwaves.com>

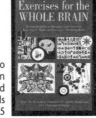